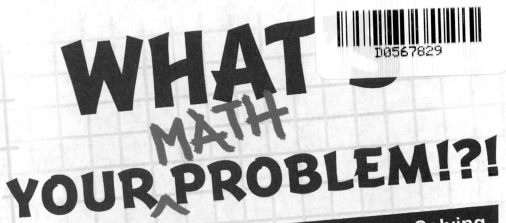

WHAT'S
MATH
YOUR PROBLEM!?!

Getting to the Heart of Teaching Problem Solving

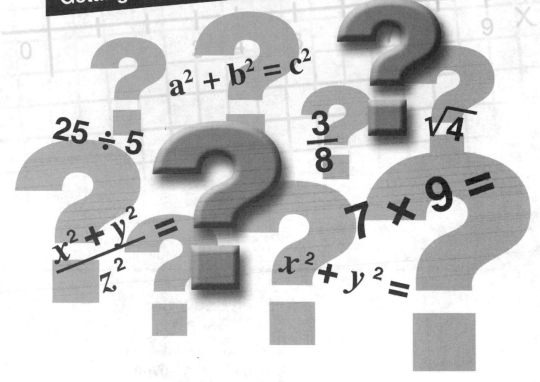

$$a^2 + b^2 = c^2$$

$$25 \div 5$$

$$\frac{3}{8}$$

$$\sqrt{4}$$

$$\frac{x^2 + y^2}{z^2} =$$

$$7 \times 9 =$$

$$x^2 + y^2 =$$

Author
Linda Gojak, M.A.Ed.

Foreword
Laney Sammons

SHELL EDUCATION

Publishing Credits

Dona Herweck Rice, *Editor-in-Chief*; Lee Aucoin, *Creative Director*; Don Tran, *Print Production Manager;* Sara Johnson, M.S.Ed., *Senior Editor;* Hillary Wolfe, *Editor*; Juan Chavolla, *Cover/Interior Layout Designer;* Corinne Burton, *M.A. Ed., Publisher*

Shell Education

5301 Oceanus Drive
Huntington Beach, CA 92649-1030
http://www.shelleducation.com
ISBN 978-1-4258-0788-7
© 2011 Shell Educational Publishing, Inc.

Table of Contents

Foreword

In 2001, the National Research Council (NRC) in its report *Adding It Up: Helping Children Learn Mathematics* warned that "too few students in our elementary and middle schools are successfully acquiring the mathematical knowledge, the skill, and the confidence they need to use the mathematics they have learned." The NRC deemed this fact to be a cause of great concern since "citizens who cannot reason mathematically are cut off from whole realms of human endeavor. Innumeracy deprives them not only of opportunity but also of competence in everyday tasks."

Our own mathematical educations too often focused on memorization, learning procedures, and computation, rather than on developing a deep conceptual understanding. Our instruction usually came from a textbook. The teacher taught procedures and students completed practice problems. Rich problem-solving experiences were the exceptions, not the rule.

The NRC's concerns led educators to examine the quality of current mathematics instruction. They found that what was missing was ample opportunities for rich, multi-layered problem-solving.

Building conceptual understanding starts with engagement. Research shows "both the curriculum and instruction should begin with problems, dilemmas, and questions for students" (Hiebert et al. 1997). When students are challenged to roll up their sleeves and delve into the messy world of mathematics, they gain mathematical perspective and understanding to be confident "everyday mathematicians."

Many teachers are searching for resources to help them effectively integrate rich problems into their mathematics lessons. This book involves students in challenges, gives strategies for solving problems, and guides teachers as they assess students' problem-solving abilities.

Include problem solving in all of the mathematical domains to teach specific content and to access the process standards set forth by the National Council of Teachers of Mathematics (2000) and the standards for mathematical practice in the Common Core State Standards for Mathematics (2010). The problem-solving framework and the Launch, Explore, Summarize Instructional Model that Gojak presents gives teachers specific structures for integrating problem-based learning in the classroom.

Novice and experienced teachers will appreciate the descriptions of the strategies. Gojak helps readers understand each strategy, shows how to use it effectively, and then gives examples of problems for application.

Use this book for professional study! Solve problems in your own journals and reflect on the experience. Use it in a study group where the conversations will provide valuable perspectives about scenarios that may arise in the classroom. As Gojak advises, "don't be surprised if some of the best ideas come from your students!"

Finally, a chapter is devoted to formative and summative assessments. Advising teachers to throw away their preconceived notions of assessment, Gojak offers specific suggestions and provides ways to effectively use the data from these assessments.

Sample problems for each strategy, sorted by grade level bands, are provided in the appendices along with templates for student problem-solving journals, rubrics, and teacher recording sheets.

What's Your Math Problem!?! Getting to the Heart of Teaching Problem Solving is a practical, teacher-friendly guide. With these strategies and resources, teachers can confidently incorporate challenging, rich problems into their mathematics lessons.

—**Laney Sammons**

Mathematics Consultant and
author of the best-selling book,
Guided Math

Acknowledgements

Thank you to those who have influenced my work, my teaching, and my belief that mathematics is so much more than learning to compute. Thank you to Johnny Hill, Jim Heddens, Dick Davies, Peggy Kasten, Steve Meiring, and Dick Little. Also, thanks to "Stash" and the thousands of students who have successfully learned that problem solving is much more rewarding than a page of long division problems!

Introduction

The purpose of this book is to help you help students be successful mathematical problem solvers. To do this, we must become more comfortable with problem solving ourselves. We need to examine our own beliefs about problem solving, how we can more effectively incorporate rich problems into our mathematics instruction, and we need to solve problems! This book presents a strategy-based approach to problem solving and models how to use the strategies effectively with students. The following strategies are discussed throughout the book:

- Restate the Problem in Your Own Words

- Identify Wanted, Given, and Needed Information

- Identify a Subgoal

- Select Appropriate Notation

- Look for a Pattern

- Create a Table

- Create an Organized List

- Guess and Check

- Make a Model

- Draw a Picture or Diagram

- Act It Out

- Create or Use a Graph

- Solve a Simpler Problem

- Account for All Possibilities

- Work Backwards

- Change Your Point of View

Chapter 1 addresses general beliefs about problem solving for students in kindergarten through grade 8. It helps present the "5 Ws and an H" behind problem solving.

Management and organizational strategies and suggestions to successfully implement problem solving into mathematics instruction appear in **Chapter 2**, along with ideas for differentiation and grouping students to best meet their needs.

Chapters 3 through 6 present an extensive—but not exhaustive—list of problem-solving strategies. Each section begins with a description of the strategy and offers suggestions for its introduction to students, followed by several sample problems. Problems are assigned a grade-level range to give you an idea of the type of task to use to help students become comfortable using the strategy. Also included are rich mathematical problems that can be solved using the strategies suggested. Work these problems in your problem-solving journal. You will become a better problem solver by solving problems! In addition you will grow professionally and become familiar with how to use each strategy. Here are a few suggestions for ways to work these problems:

- **Alone:** Spend as much time as you need. The solutions shown are only suggestions. Rich problems often have several solution methods.

- **As part of a professional study group:** Work your way through the book with your colleagues. Solve the problems and discuss your thinking. Or, assign problems to your students and use the study group to review and discuss student work.

- **As professional development:** The strategies and problems in this book can be used in a class or professional development workshop.

Although suggestions are included with the strategies, explanations, and solutions, the best way you can learn and grow from this work is to make it your own. Compare your solution process with mine. Compare your students' work with your work.

In Chapter 7, assessment is addressed with suggestions for how to informally and formally assess students' mathematical reasoning and understanding.

Chapter 8 includes answers to the most frequently asked questions about problem solving from teachers around the world that I have met over the years in professional development settings.

Reflection questions are included in every chapter to encourage you to think about your own beliefs about problem solving. Include your reflections in your problem-solving journal as you journey through this book and answer them as you read. As you implement some of these ideas with your students, reread your reflections. Are you thinking differently about any of these ideas, or are your beliefs reinforced? Most of all, enjoy your problem-solving journal. Use drawings, markers, tables, and charts! Organize it in a way that is most useful to you. Refer back to it often and extend it beyond the problems in this book. As you continue on the road to professional growth, you will find new ideas and more problems to solve. And, don't be surprised if some of the best ideas come from your students!

Happy problem solving!

—Linda Gojak

CHAPTER 1

The 5 Ws and an H of Problem Solving

"Problem solving develops the belief in students that they are capable of doing mathematics and that mathematics makes sense."

Van de Walle et al. 2009

Stop and Think

Respond to the questions below in your problem-solving journal.

- Think back to your own experience as a student. What do you recall about solving problems?
- What is your definition of a good problem?

What Is Problem Solving?

Do you recall "doing story problems" in mathematics? They usually applied the computation and skill practice from the text book. There was little critical thinking involved to determine what you were supposed to do with the numbers contained in the problem. Not much has changed in today's mathematics textbooks. For example, after the lesson on multiplication, there might be 15 multiplication exercises for practice, followed by three or four word problems, at least one of which is an application of multiplication.

These "problems" serve the purpose of giving students practice using computational skills in a context or a situation. However, they do not help students to develop a deeper understanding of the concept behind the skill. This deeper understanding, referred to as *conceptual understanding*, involves more than applying isolated facts or procedures. Research on learning mathematics suggests that we learn new ideas in mathematics by making connections to ideas we already understand and extending the new ideas to novel situations. This is the development of conceptual understanding. For example, what is really happening when you multiply 9 by 28? You demonstrate procedural knowledge when you can go through the steps of multiplying and reaching a product of 216. Conceptual knowledge involves understanding that 9×28 means you have "nine groups with 28 items in each group." You can demonstrate conceptual knowledge using words, pictures, models, or numbers. When students repeat the procedure demonstrated by the teacher, they develop the skill of multiplication. When students develop an understanding of what multiplication means *beyond* the procedure, they can apply that understanding to a variety of situations that call for multiplication.

Routine problems, or traditional "story problems" involve situations in which the learner knows how to solve the problem based on past experiences. In solving routine problems, the learner reproduces and applies a known procedure. Problem solved!

Non-routine problems and rich mathematical tasks involve situations in which the learner does not immediately know how to reach a solution. The learner must draw upon his or her comprehension of a variety of mathematical concepts and then select and extend that understanding to develop an approach that leads to a reasonable solution. The level of rigor in non-routine problems is much greater than in traditional problems. Students must grapple with the mathematics they know, extending and applying it in a new context.

Principles and Standards for School Mathematics (NCTM 2000) defines problem solving as "engaging in a task for which the solution method is not known in advance. In order to find a solution, students must draw on their knowledge, and through this process, they will develop new mathematical understandings. Solving problems is both a goal of learning mathematics and a major means of doing so. Students need frequent opportunities to formulate, grapple with, and solve complex problems that require a significant amount of effort and should then be encouraged to reflect on their thinking."

Here are examples of a routine and a non-routine problem.

Example 1

Marsha wants to fill a rectangular box with centimeter cubes. The box is 8 cm high, 4 cm wide and 6 cm deep. How many cubes will fit in the box?

Example 2

You have taken a job at the "We Box It" company, which makes cardboard boxes of different shapes and sizes for packaging and shipping products. You and your partner are in charge of boxing "fidgets," which are cube-shaped filters that are placed inside aquariums to filter the water. Fidgets are packed into larger boxes for shipping to pet stores. Here are some of the shipping boxes:

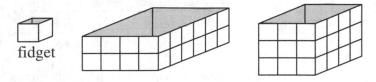
fidget

You need to pack 36 fidgets into a box. What size boxes could you use? Which box would be the best to use? Why?

Take some time to solve each of these problems. As you work on them, think about which requires procedural knowledge and which develops conceptual knowledge.

Solution to Example 1: You likely solved this problem by applying the formula, length × width × height (or depth) to the numbers given in the problem ($8 \times 4 \times 6 = 192$). Of course, the final solution must be labeled cubic centimeters, although many students have no idea of why that is the unit used to measure volume.

Solution to Example 2: One way to solve this problem is to count 36 cubes and build the boxes that could be used. Students may draw pictures to represent their boxes. You could organize their work in a table similar to the one shown below.

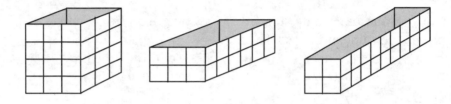

Length	Width	Height
1	1	36
1	2	18
1	3	12
1	4	9
1	6	6
2	2	9
2	3	6
3	3	4

However, the mathematics doesn't stop when the table is complete. Classroom discussion can focus on which box would be best to use—and why.

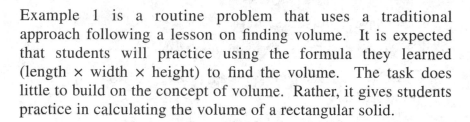

Respond to the question below in your problem-solving journal.

- What mathematical concepts are developed in the fidget problem?

Example 1 is a routine problem that uses a traditional approach following a lesson on finding volume. It is expected that students will practice using the formula they learned (length × width × height) to find the volume. The task does little to build on the concept of volume. Rather, it gives students practice in calculating the volume of a rectangular solid.

Example 2 is a non-routine or "rich" problem developing the concept of volume. In this problem students are given a situation in which they need to build an understanding of volume in order to complete the task. When solving this problem, students develop an understanding of volume by determining which three-dimensional boxes will hold 36 cubes. This is called the *volume* of the box. They discuss the various ways they found the dimensions and how they know they have all of the possibilities. Notice that this problem is likely to include a conversation about whether a box that has a length of 2, a width of 2 and a height of 9 (2 by 2 by 9) is the same as a box with the dimensions $9 \times 2 \times 2$. This idea connects to the concept of the commutative property of multiplication. The discussion will eventually conclude with students discovering that multiplying the length times the width times the height will give the volume of a rectangular prism (box).

When first faced with a problem such as the fidget problem, students may struggle because they are unfamiliar with how to approach such a task. That makes it a real problem. The role of the teacher is to be aware of the mathematical understandings developed in each problem we give our students as well as how we can support their thinking without simply showing them what to do.

In general, rich mathematical tasks or problems have the following characteristics:

- involve substantial mathematics
- have multiple points of entry
- can be solved in a variety of ways
- can have multiple solutions
- promote discussion and communication
- involve students in interpreting, testing, proving, explaining, and reflecting
- implicitly intrigue and motivate students
- can be scaffolded to meet the individual needs of students
- help to develop conceptual understanding of mathematical ideas

Stop and Think

Respond to the questions below in your problem-solving journal.

- Why is problem solving an important part of teaching and learning mathematics?
- How does problem solving support mathematical reasoning?

Why Teach Problem Solving?

The National Council of Teachers of Mathematics in *Principles and Standards for School Mathematics* (2001) recognizes problem solving to be "an integral part of all mathematics learning, and so it should not be an isolated part of the mathematics program. Problem solving in mathematics should involve all five content areas. The contexts of the problems can vary from familiar experiences involving students' lives or the school day to applications involving the sciences or the world of work. Good problems will integrate multiple topics and will involve significant mathematics." Additionally, the other process standards—communication, connections, reasoning and proof, and representations—provide a platform for teaching problem solving. It is through these process standards that students work to make sense of and apply mathematical content.

In addition to problem solving, the process standards include communication, connections, representation, reasoning, and proof. Let's take a look at each of these processes to illustrate how they support problem solving in and out of the classroom.

Communication

The process standard of Communication involves reading, writing, talking about, and listening to others' ideas about mathematics. As students approach rich tasks and good problems, they must be able to read the problems and translate them into situations that make sense to them. They need to share ideas and strategies with others by explaining their thinking and conclusions both orally and in writing. Through class discussions, students clarify their own thinking by sharing their ideas and listening to the ideas of classmates.

Connections

The process standard for Connections includes recognizing and developing relationships among mathematical ideas. Think about the fidget problem you solved earlier. Connections between the meanings of area and volume by finding the area of the base and multiplying it by the height of the box help students use what they know to develop a strategy for finding the volume. The relationship between the commutative property and the factors of each possibility narrowed the number of possible solutions. For example, the volume of a box that is $9 \times 2 \times 2$ is the same as the volume of a box that is $2 \times 9 \times 2$. Connections are made to the units of measure used to find volume (cubic units) and why we need to measure three-dimensional space with three-dimensional units. Selecting and justifying the best box to use connects the problem to a real-world situation and provides a purpose for learning and doing mathematics.

Representation

"The ways in which mathematical ideas are represented is fundamental to how students understand and use those ideas" (NCTM 2001). There are a variety of ways students can represent their thinking as they solve problems. Pictures, words, models, tables, graphs, and numbers are among the representations used by students at all levels. Students moving from the elementary to the middle grades become more facile with symbolic representations (numbers, variables, equations) as they begin to think and reason more abstractly.

Reasoning and Proof

The process standard for Reasoning and Proof includes developing mathematical ideas, exploring phenomena, justifying results, and developing mathematical conjectures. As students solve problems, they communicate and represent their thinking, using reasoning and proof to develop and justify their thinking and solution process. They use connections to draw conclusions.

Rigorous tasks give students the opportunity to develop a deeper understanding of mathematical content through including all of the process standards. It is not a matter of choosing between content and process. Learning and doing mathematics involves both content and process. Consider the two problems involving volume that you solved earlier. Which one gives students better opportunities to reason and draw conclusions about the volume of a rectangular solid?

The NCTM Process Standards

Problem Solving

Students tackle rich tasks and problems that require them to draw on prior knowledge, employ strategies, and develop new mathematical understanding. Such tasks are thoughtfully selected, presented, and summarized so that students develop mathematical habits of mind such as persistence, curiosity, and confidence.

Communication

Students share their mathematical thinking and learn from the mathematical thinking of others; ideas are communicated in various ways, including speaking, writing, listening, drawing, and the use of manipulatives.

Connections

Students are encouraged and expected to recognize and explore the interrelatedness of mathematical ideas; the connections between mathematics and other subjects; and the relevance of mathematics to their everyday lives.

Representation

Students explore and use various ways to represent their mathematical thinking by using words, pictures, models, graphical displays, symbols including numbers and variables, expressions and equations.

Reasoning and Proof

Students make conjectures and develop ideas, including encouraging students to explain, clarify, justify, defend, and revise their thinking.

Mathematics Is Everywhere

The negative attitudes of many adults toward mathematics are likely due to the fact that they were not very successful learning mathematics. If the mathematics they did was based on drill and practice with no connection to the importance of it in our daily lives, it is no wonder that they are not excited about the possibilities mathematics offers us. We use mathematical problem solving in our daily lives. Determining the mileage my car gets is an example of using mathematics. Looking at the finance rates and deciding whether to refinance my house involves mathematics. Knowing how much fabric to purchase for the seat cushions I want to re-cover requires mathematics. In addition to the application of mathematics in our daily lives, most careers involve mathematics as well.

In the Common Core State Standards for mathematics (2010), the standards for mathematical practice describe the expertise that all mathematics educators should develop in their students. The first of these standards is to "make sense of problems and persevere in solving them." Students need to explain the meaning of a problem to themselves and look for entry points to its solution. Providing students with experiences using a variety of strategies will help to provide that entry. Thinking about the process and ideas that are used to solve a problem are as important as the solution. Thinking should not stop when the problem is solved. Looking for other ways to solve the problem or other possible solutions often leads to new discoveries and conjectures. With this approach, the students take an active role in learning and applying mathematical ideas, and the teacher orchestrates the process.

Problem solving is a key reason for learning mathematics. It is through problem solving that we can look at a situation, analyze it, and determine possible solution paths and reasonable solutions. It is problem solving that makes mathematics meaningful in our daily lives.

Respond to the question below in your problem-solving journal.

- Consider the work of an artist, a dentist, or an airplane pilot. How is mathematics used in each of those careers?

Who Should Solve Problems?

Problem solving is part of our everyday life. Consider these common daily scenarios:

- Do I take this route to work or is traffic backed up? Should I go a different way?

- Is the large box of soap a better deal than two smaller boxes?

- Do I have enough gasoline in the car to get home, or should I stop to fill up the tank?

- How do I adjust a recipe that serves 10 for my family of six?

Beyond our personal lives, we are often faced with decisions that must be influenced by our ability to reason quantitatively. What is the best site for the new community playground? How will our school district convince voters to pass a new school issue on the ballot this fall? With the advances in technology and the media, now more than ever we will all need to be informed problem solvers in order to make intelligent decisions that impact every aspect of our lives. In short, everyone needs to be able to solve problems every day.

Students should begin solving problems in preschool using experiences such as *how many blocks can I stack before my tower falls over?* By kindergarten, problem solving should be an integral part of classroom activities. Primary level students become interested in mathematics through solving interesting problems. The use of concrete materials and methods for organizing ideas are modeled by the teacher and eventually become part of the student's problem solving "toolbox." With this solid foundation, students in the upper elementary grades use more sophisticated approaches to solving problems and, through a variety of experiences, should represent their thinking in written and oral formats. Middle-grade students build upon earlier experiences and make connections to algebraic and geometric representations. Through many opportunities to solve rich problems, students become adept at determining how to get started with a problem and how to follow through with a solution process that not only supplies a correct answer but also enables students to draw upon that process when solving similar problems.

Although all levels of students should be solving problems, not all problem-solving strategies are developmentally appropriate for all levels of students. The chart on the following page recommends which strategy to use at each grade level. This can change based on students' readiness levels, but should be used as a guide.

Strategy	K-2	3-5	6-8
Restate the Problem in Your Own Words	X	X	X
Identify Wanted, Given, and Needed Information		X	X
Identify a Subgoal		X	X
Select Appropriate Notation	X	X	X
Look for a Pattern	X	X	X
Create a Table	X	X	X
Create an Organized List		X	X
Guess and Check	X	X	X
Make a Model	X	X	X
Draw a Picture or Diagram	X	X	X
Act It Out	X	X	X
Create or Use a Graph		X	X
Solve a Simpler Problem		X	X
Account for All Possibilities		X	X
Work Backwards		X	X
Change Your Point of View		X	X

Teachers also need to be purposeful about the problems and tasks assigned to students. Much like the saying "a picture is worth a thousand words," with problem solving, one good problem is worth a thousand division exercises!

Appropriate content, possible strategies, reasonable solutions, and the ability to tweak a problem to meet the needs of a variety of students are all critical components of effective instruction. We become better problem solvers by solving problems ourselves! Many of us never learned to do mathematics in this way. It is critical that students have many opportunities and a variety of problems to solve to learn mathematics in a way that is meaningful and sensible.

Stop and Think

Respond to the question below in your problem-solving journal.

- How often do your students solve problems?

When Should We Solve Problems?

Problem solving should be a part of every mathematics class. If students are to appreciate mathematics, they need to be involved with doing mathematics and applying mathematics. Helping students to understand a concept through problem solving also helps them to develop number sense. Consider this problem:

Patty answered the following test item as shown below. Is she correct? If so, explain how you know that her answer is correct. If not, convince her why her answer is incorrect.

$$\frac{1}{2} + \frac{2}{3} = \frac{3}{5}$$

There are many ways you can include more problem solving in your instruction. Some suggestions with examples are shown in the charts on the following pages. Keep in mind that a problem does not have to include words if you frame a rich classroom conversation around the mathematics. This list will get you started thinking about how you can include more problem solving in your classroom everyday.

Here are some suggestions for the times when problem solving could occur throughout the day.

Time to Use	Focus	Examples
Morning Meeting (K–2)	• Discussions about mathematics in a variety of situations.	• Calendar Math • Number of the Day
Learning Centers	• Games, activities, and problems that students can do independently or in small groups with minimal teacher involvement.	• How many ways can you make change for a quarter? • How many ways can you make change for a dollar?
Warm-up/ Review	• Problems on the board for students to solve at the beginning of class, including some discussion of the problems so students can use this as a learning experience if they are still struggling with the concept.	• Sara wrote the following on her mathematics test: $$\frac{1}{2} + \frac{3}{4} = \frac{4}{6}$$ Convince her that her response is correct or incorrect.

The chart on the following pages offers some examples of the times in a lesson where problem solving could be used:

Time to Use	Focus	Examples
Introduce a Concept	• Help students to make sense out of a concept that the class is preparing to study.	• Build all the rectangular puppy pens that you can, using 16 feet of fencing.
Introduce Strategies	• Provide formal modeling and instruction in order to use problem-solving strategies.	• Introduce making an organized list: *Martina has three shirts, two pairs of shorts, and three pairs of shoes. How many different outfits can she wear?*
Group Work	• Allow students to work together to complete a task by sharing ideas and understandings.	• Work together to solve a problem and share your solutions with the class using poster paper or a document camera.
Assessment	• Use a rich problem that focuses on student understanding of a concept. This can be formative or summative assessment.	• Assess student understanding of subtraction from 100: *You have a bag with 100 pennies. Reach in and remove a handful of pennies. Determine how many pennies are left in the bag.*

Time to Use	Focus	Examples
Connect to Other Subjects	• Use mathematics explicitly in other subjects.	• Collect and organize data in science: *Given a list of the areas of 10 states, place those states in order from largest to smallest.*
Homework	• Assign one rich problem rather than a set of exercises.	• Following a class task on division of whole numbers, assign the following problem: *Find the missing digits:* $$8) \overline{1\,\square,5\,\square 8} \quad \square,5\,\square 1$$
Problem of the Week	• Use learned strategies to solve rich problems, with adequate time to explore possible solution strategies and to represent work in an organized way.	• Following some work with the Make a Table strategy, students work in groups: *Find all the ways to make change for a quarter.*

Time to Use	Focus	Examples
Interactive Whiteboard Technology	• Get students motivated and engaged with this technology.	• Manipulate "outfits": *You have one yellow, one red, and one blue shirt. How many different outfits can you make if you have one pair each of blue pants and black pants?* • Discuss using patterns and other methods of solving the problem.
Developing Number Sense	• Encourage the development of number sense as a concept is being taught or reviewed; include discussions about an answer's reasonableness.	• Which of the following numbers does not belong in this list? *9, 16, 36, 48, 64, 81* • Explain your thinking.
Differentiation	• Adjust problems for students who need extra support or extra challenge.	• You have nickels, dimes and quarters. *How many nickels make change for a quarter?* *Find three ways to make change for 50¢.* *Find four ways to make change for $1.00.*

Time to Use	Focus	Examples
Connect to Children's Literature	• Introduce a problem as a follow-up activity to a story or book that students have read.	• After reading *Equal Shmequal* by Virginia Kroll (2005): *Solve the following and explain your thinking.* $3 + 7 =$ ___ $+ 3$ ___ $= 7 + 8$ $5 + 7 =$ ___ $+ 7$
Bulletin Board Activity	• Display a problem or activity on the bulletin board with an envelope for student solutions; post some responses. Change the bulletin board regularly.	• Complete the patterns. *1, 3, 5,* ___, ___, ___, *13* *3, 6, 9,* ___, ___, ___ *1, 1, 2, 3, 5, 8,* ___, ___, ___

Respond to the question below in your problem-solving journal.

- What are some ways that you can incorporate more problem solving into your mathematics lessons?

How Should We Teach Problem Solving?

There are many ways that problem solving can be incorporated into mathematics instruction. Envision students using a rich problem as a way to apply the mathematical concept that was just taught in a lesson and solving a related problem in small groups. This enables these students to understand the real-world connection to that mathematical concept and find a practical solution that is relevant and important to them. Consider using a problem as a vehicle through which to demonstrate a mathematical concept to the entire class. While grappling with the problem as a class, students are presented with the lesson's main objective.

Finally, with NCTM's description in mind, consider another approach to incorporating problem solving into mathematics instruction. Imagine a lesson that begins with a problem as a context to help students uncover the mathematics for that day. Students work together in small groups to explore, trying a variety of strategies and approaches to reach a reasonable solution. More importantly, as the class comes together to share and discuss their approaches, they solidify their understanding of the mathematics in the problem. The teacher becomes the one who orchestrates the discussion through thoughtful questioning.

Where Can You Find Good Problems?

There are many resources for good problems in a variety of formats. You can find traditional problems and turn them into rich problems. Playing a game that requires the use of mathematical reasoning is problem solving. Analyzing a mathematical situation to determine what is a reasonable solution is also problem solving.

- If you have an opportunity to attend a professional meeting such as a National Council of Teachers of Mathematics national or regional meeting or your state mathematics council meeting, check the exhibit hall for good problem-solving resources.

- Visit your local library. The games section usually includes problems, often described as games or puzzles, that you can easily adjust for use with your students. Picture books and other examples of children's literature also make good topics for writing your own problems. There are also many books available that include using children's literature in the classroom. One such source is NCTM's publications. Another online source is the Ohio Resource Center (**http://ohiorc.org/for/math/bookshelf/default.aspx**).

Online resources can vary in quality. Some excellent resources include:

- *Illuminations* (**http://illuminations.nctm.org/**)—This site includes lessons, activities, and other links that are sorted by grade level and mathematical concept. Some of the activities are applets that can be done at home or over the summer.

- *PBS Mathline* (**http://www.pbs.org/teachers/classroom/prek/math/resources/**)—This site is for pre-K teachers, but the menu at the top of the page allows access to other grade levels. This site includes problems, problem-based lessons, and even some classroom video of the lessons being taught. It is a great place to get started!

- *Annenberg Media* (**http://www.learner.org/**)—
  This site offers a variety of rich mathematical tasks by grade band. There are also some online courses that you can take to become more familiar with the process standards for each grade level band (K–2, 3–5, 6–8).

- *Calculation Nation* (**http://calculationnation.nctm.org/**)—
  Calculation Nation® uses the power of the Internet to let students challenge opponents from anywhere in the world. At the same time, students are able to challenge themselves by investigating significant mathematical content and practicing fundamental skills. The element of competition adds an extra layer of excitement.

Reflect and Act

Respond to the questions below in your problem-solving journal.

1. How is problem solving an important part of your professional growth as a mathematics educator?

2. How can you convince your students of the importance of problem solving when learning mathematics?

3. Think about problems you solved in this chapter that involved quantitative reasoning. Write a description of how you went about approaching and determining a reasonable solution.

4. How has your perspective of problem solving changed after reading this chapter?

CHAPTER 2

Planning for Problem Solving in the Classroom

"A teacher's goal must be to help students understand mathematics; yet understanding is not something that one can teach directly. No matter how kindly, clearly, patiently, or slowly teachers explain, they cannot make *students understand. Understanding takes place in students' minds as they connect new information with previously developed ideas, and teaching through problem solving is a powerful way to promote this kind of thinking."*

Lester 2003

As you think about planning a rich problem-solving lesson, think about why so many students struggle with problem solving. What is different about the thinking that goes into the typical mathematics task such as 28 × 32 and solving a problem involving finding the possible dimensions of a playground that covers 896 square yards? As we plan for teaching students how to solve rich problems, it is important for us to understand the different kind of learning that is required to approach each of these tasks and how we can help students to be successful beyond developing computational skills.

Students often struggle with problems because they do not have a framework for approaching these tasks. For many students, experience in mathematics consists of doing numerical computations. They learn a procedure, apply it to calculate the answer, and the work is complete.

Solving problems involves more than following a procedure. The student must attach meaning to the problem, decide on steps that will help lead to a solution, follow those steps—possibly revising them along the way—and finally determine if the solution is reasonable. This is certainly much more complicated than calculating the product of 28×32!

Setting up a positive problem-solving classroom requires planning for successful instruction, which leads to positive experiences for your students.

Finding a Good Problem

It is important to start by finding a good problem for your students to solve. Look back at the characteristics of rich mathematical problems in the chart in Chapter 1. Keep these characteristics in mind as you consider which problems to use with your students. Find a problem that has the mathematical concepts you want to teach embedded in the solution process. For example, if today's lesson is on equivalent fractions, look for a problem that helps students construct the meaning of equivalent fractions as part of the solution process.

If your students have not had much experience with solving rich problems, you also need to consider the difficulty level of the problem you select. The problem must be "doable" for the students. At the same time, it should offer rich mathematics for the students to grapple with. If it is too simple, students will not get the value of learning new mathematics. If it is too difficult, students will become frustrated and give up. Either way, you have not accomplished your goal of building students' problem-solving abilities.

There are many websites with rich problems (see pages 35–36) as well as other professional resources that include various problems at different grade levels. Start slowly. Choose a few good problems that align with your curriculum and begin to build a problem-solving library. Share problems with your colleagues.

Each of the next chapters includes problems to help you get started. There are also additional practice problems provided in Appendix C.

As you build your problem-solving library, you will also become more comfortable modifying problems. Something as simple as using the names of students in your class will increase the motivation to solve the problem. Putting the situation in a context that is of interest to your students such as sports, humor, or games also adds to the motivational element. Consider the following problem, which falls into the category of "fractured fairy tales." Students love it. It is intrinsically interesting and motivational— not to mention just plain silly!

> Pinocchio had a habit of telling lies. Each time he told a lie, his nose would grow. One morning while working at his father's clock shop, Pinocchio decided to see just how long he could make his nose. He measured his nose at its original length and found it was 2 inches long. Then he yelled out, "Dogs make the best brain surgeons!" His nose grew 3 inches! He shouted, "Chocolate is the best toothpaste!" Again, his nose grew 3 inches longer. He stood on the table and hollered, "Going to school makes you dumb!" Out went his nose…another 3 inches! After Pinocchio had told 15 lies, how long was his nose?

Keep in mind that a good task takes time to solve. In fact, it is not unusual for a good problem to take several days/class periods. Remember, students are not just doing an exercise in mathematics or practicing a skill. Rich problems give students opportunities to learn new mathematics or to deepen their current knowledge of mathematical ideas. This takes time. However, you will see that the learning that takes place is well worth the time investment. As we look at the following instructional model that is helpful in planning, we will consider how the issue of time can be addressed.

A Problem-Solving Framework

George Polya, a 20th century mathematician, was a great advocate for the use of problem-solving techniques in learning mathematics. His most famous book, *How To Solve It*, was first published in 1945. Since then it has sold over a million copies and is still in publication today.

In *How To Solve It*, Polya identifies four principles of problem solving. These principles provide a framework to help students approach any type of problem. Interestingly, Polya's principles can also be applied to problems outside of mathematics and are often applied in doing science-related activities.

Principle One: Understand the Problem

Too often students jump into solving a problem without considering all of the details and any special situations. What does understanding a problem entail? How do you know when you understand the problem? More importantly, how do we ensure that a student knows when he understands the problem he is trying to solve?

This principle includes several of the problem-solving strategies from the later chapters of this book. They are as follows:

- Restate the Problem in Your Own Words

- Identify Wanted, Given, and Needed Information

- Identify a Subgoal

- Draw a Picture or Diagram

- Select Appropriate Notation

Although there is no particular order to the strategies used to recognize all of the essential details in a problem, each is an important step in comprehending the problem. Students should begin by reading the problem and restating it in their own words. Visualizing the problem will help to focus on the important details. Make students aware that it often takes more than one reading to identify the critical details. Identifying the wanted, given, and needed information includes focusing on the question asked to begin to consider how to get started and what to do. What data do I have? What is unknown? What am I looking for to reach a solution? Students also must understand whether the problem involves multiple steps and if a subgoal must be identified. Drawing a picture or diagram can add to the understanding of what is given and, at the same time, can help to focus on what is needed to solve the problem. Also consider the type of notation to use, which may be modeling with concrete materials to using mathematical symbols that will be helpful in getting started on the problem.

Respond to the questions below in your problem-solving journal.

- Choose a rich problem that you have used with students in the past or that you would like to use with them. Think about how you developed an understanding of the problem.

- What steps did you take to make sense of the situation to help you get started?

Principle Two: Devise a Plan

Now that you have a clearer understanding of the problem situation, it is time to consider how you will go about solving it. It may be simple calculations that will enable you to reach a solution. For many students, determining which mathematical operation to use presents a challenge. This is often because they have not associated meaning with the facts of the problem and the question being asked, or they do not have a deep understanding of the meaning of the operation and depend on "key words" (which don't work!) to tell them what to do.

Rigorous problems often involve more than one or two computational steps. You have to determine how to get started, what approach may lead to a successful solution, and how you will represent your thinking in order to carry out your plan. This is where the problem-solving strategies come in. It is a good idea to have a list of the strategies available for students to consider every time they solve a problem. Think about which of the strategies may be helpful. Too often, students do not take the time to think about appropriate strategies before they begin to attempt a solution.

Once you have determined which strategies will help you to get started, think about how you will relate the information in the problem to using the strategies. If you decide that making a table will help you use the information in the problem, you need to consider what information should be used in the table. If you choose to solve a simpler problem first, how will you modify the problem so you can get started? How will you use the information to determine if there is a pattern you can complete to reach the original solution?

Stop and Think

Respond to the questions below in your problem-solving journal.

Look back at the problem you selected on page 44.

- What strategies did you decide to use?

- How did you choose those strategies?

Principle Three: Carry out the Plan

Once you have decided which strategies to use, it is time to implement the plan. An important part of this principle is to check each step as you proceed. Asking yourself questions throughout the solution process will help you to know if you are headed in a direction that is leading towards an acceptable solution or if you must change your course. Sometimes you will get started and find you need to change your approach by adjusting a strategy, adding more strategies, or selecting an entirely different approach. This is all part of learning to be a problem solver. Although this can be frustrating for students, it is also what provides the satisfaction of reaching the solution and understanding the steps and effort it took to get there!

An important part of learning and doing mathematics is making sense out of the work that you have done. Keeping an accurate representation of your work is fundamental to making sense out of the mathematical ideas that have developed from the solution process. Representation and communication help you to clarify your thinking and identify connections to other mathematical ideas and to real-life applications. The solution process, which is the way you carry out your plan, leads to a deeper level of understanding and enables you to apply that knowledge to new and different situations.

Stop and Think

Respond to the questions below in your problem-solving journal.

Look back at the problem you selected on page 44.

- How did you carry out your plan?

- Did you need to adapt, add, or change strategies?

- Is your written work (*representation*) an accurate record of what you did?

- How does it help you to develop a deeper understanding of the mathematical ideas that emerged from the problem?

Principle Four: Look Back

It is not uncommon for students to solve a problem, close their book, and be finished. This stage involves several steps. Consider your results in light of the data in the original problem and ask yourself the following questions:

- Does my solution make sense?

- Is my solution reasonable?

- Does my solution fit all of the conditions of the problem?

However, looking back involves more than just checking to see if the solution is reasonable. Polya (1945) states, "A good teacher should understand and impress on his students the view that no problem whatever is completely exhausted. There remains always something to do; . . . we could improve any solution, and, in any case, we can always improve our understanding of the solution."

As you plan problem-solving experiences for your students, consider possible connections that students will make by solving and sharing their solution processes. Recognizing relationships among the mathematics in problems helps students to develop mathematical understandings. It is Polya's *Look Back* principle that provides students with the opportunity to dig deeper by taking the time to ask themselves if there are other possible solutions to the problem and if there are other approaches to reaching a solution.

Launch, Explore, Summarize Instructional Model

Putting this all together for students can be quite overwhelming. Developing lessons that incorporate problem solving to teach a new concept or to supplement your current instruction requires a different mindset for planning. The Launch, Explore, Summarize Instructional Model incorporates rich problems, Polya's principles, and effective student learning.

The Launch, Explore, Summarize Instructional Model was first developed and used in the research of William Fitzgerald and Jan Schroyer (1986). It has become very helpful language in which to organize a discussion around teaching a lesson, investigation, and unit.

Teaching through problem solving does not mean giving students a rich problem or task and waiting for them to come up with a solution. The teacher is the key to providing the students with the information, techniques, questions, and ultimately habits of mind that lead to successful mathematics experiences both within and outside the classroom. The Launch, Explore, Summarize Instructional Model defines a lesson in three parts. Read on for a closer look at what each part entails and how the model can be used to plan a successful problem-solving lesson.

Launch

Launching the lesson engages the students in the problem they are to solve. In the Launch phase, the teacher prepares the class for the problem by reviewing any previously learned concepts that may be connected to the mathematics in the problem. In order for students to have an entry into a problem, they must understand the context of the problem. It is also during this part of the lesson that students complete the first of Polya's principles by making sense of the problem situation and the facts in the problem. By the end of the Launch, students should be well into Polya's second principle, with a plan for getting started. The length of the Launch should be relatively short (up to 10 minutes). If it is too long, there will not be enough time for the Explore and Summarize phases of the lesson.

Questions to Consider when Planning the Launch

The following questions will help you think about what you need to consider as you plan how you will launch the problem:

- What prior knowledge do students need to solve this problem?

- How will I review these concepts and help students to connect them to the problem?

- Have students had prior experience with the context of the problem? If not, how will I present this context?

- How can I make the problem personal and motivating for students? How can I introduce the problem without giving away too much information?

- What student misconceptions may arise in understanding and solving the problem? How will I deal with students' misconceptions without telling them what to do?

- How long do I anticipate it will take students to solve the problem?

- What scaffolding will help struggling students? What extensions will challenge students who are able to solve the problem?

The order of the questions is not important. In fact, you may find that they are closely connected, so while considering one planning question, you are addressing other questions as well. For example, as you consider whether students understand the context of the problem, you may also be thinking about how you can tweak it to make it more interesting and motivating.

Take a look at the problem on the following page that could be used with second graders. As you read through the list of questions following the problem, think about each question in terms of using this with a second-grade class. Remember, the more experiences you have selecting and planning to launch a problem with your students, the better you (and your students) will get. It can be time consuming at first, but before long this kind of planning will become inherent in all of your problem-solving lessons.

What prior knowledge do students need to solve this problem?

> Moira bought a pencil for 29¢. She gave the clerk a dollar bill and received five coins in change. What coins did she receive?

Consider the mathematics you want students to do as you select the problem. Think about how students will get started. Sometimes the problem is so straightforward that they can jump right in. Other problems require prerequisite knowledge in order to reach a solution.

Stop and Think

Respond to the questions below in your problem-solving journal.

- What prerequisite knowledge would a student need in order to solve this problem?
- Make a list in your journal. Talk with your colleagues about the problem and the lists you each developed.

How will I review these concepts and help students to connect them to the problem?

Now that you have the list of prerequisite concepts and knowledge the students need, you should consider how to provide a quick review so that students have entry into the problem. Consider the experience level of your students as you decide what you need to review before starting the problem.

Using the problem above in a second-grade class, consider students' experience with subtraction and recognizing coins. These concepts will also help you to determine differentiation needs of the students. Students who cannot subtract will need more scaffolding than those who can.

Respond to the question below in your problem-solving journal.

- How would you review the prerequisite skills needed to solve the problem above with a class of second-graders?

Have students had prior experience with the context of the problem? If not, how will I present this context?

Consider the previous experiences of your students prior to presenting a problem to them. If they have little or no experience with the situation presented in the problem, think about ways that you can expose them to it. For example, if urban students have had little or no experience gardening, a problem in which they must find the perimeter of a fence that is to go around a garden will have little meaning to them. You might introduce the problem above by talking about going to the store and getting change and simulating the exchange using yourself and student volunteers. Some suggestions include showing a short video clip, reading a book, showing some pictures, or creating the situation in the classroom. Your introduction should be broad enough to help students picture the context of the problem without giving too much information.

Stop and Think

Respond to the questions below in your problem-solving journal.

- Think about how students might visualize the context of a problem. What questions would you ask? Would you tell a short story? Is there a book that you could use to set the stage for your students?

How can I make the problem personal and motivating for students? How can I introduce the problem without giving away too much information?

This question relates to the previous question in that setting the context can also get the students excited about solving the problem. Using student names in the problem, setting it up in the context of a game that the students like to play, a television show, a cartoon character, or a rock band will spark student interest.

Be careful when you introduce the problem not to give the students so much information that they do not have to think about how to solve the problem on their own.

Respond to the direction below in your problem-solving journal.

- How could your rewrite the problem to present a situation that would motivate a class of second graders to work on finding a solution?

What student misconceptions may arise in understanding and solving the problem? How will I deal with students' misconceptions without telling them what to do?

As you think of the mathematics in the problem, be aware of areas that might be difficult for students. Consider if it is the mathematics that might trip them up or if an issue could arise from not being able to understand the problem. If it is the mathematics, you will need to be ready to scaffold the problem. If it is comprehension, anticipate questions that you might ask to clarify student understanding.

Respond to the questions below in your problem-solving journal.

- Which mathematical ideas in the problem might students struggle with? What questions can you ask to address those misconceptions? What comprehension difficulties might students have? How will you help students to deal with those misunderstandings?

How long do I anticipate it will take students to solve the problem?

Ideally students should be able to complete all three parts of the lesson (Launch, Explore, Summarize) in one class period. However, not all rich problems are designed to be solved in a given amount of time. You need to consider this as you select problems to use with your students. Do you need to finish the entire lesson in one day? Can you launch the problem and allow students to get started on it and come back to it tomorrow (or even in a few days)? For students who are just starting with problem solving and using strategies, consider problems that will take a class period. Once they become comfortable with the strategies and have developed the tenacity to stick with a problem—even when they are stuck—you will want to add more challenging problems that will take several days to solve.

What scaffolding will help struggling students? What extensions will challenge students who are able to solve the problem?

As you put all of the pieces together for the launch part of the lesson, you need to consider differentiating for various student levels. After you have considered the mathematics in the problem you have selected and anticipated possible misconceptions, begin to think about how you can adjust the lesson for the students who are struggling with the problem, who have the right idea but have some computational errors, who can do the mathematics but struggle with reading comprehension, and who can solve the problem with little difficulty and are ready for more!

It is important to consider this question in advance. At first, it will take some time to think about the problem in terms of all of your students' needs. After some practice, it does become much easier and you will find that problem-based lessons are an excellent way to meet individual needs in the classroom.

Stop and Think

Respond to the questions below in your problem-solving journal.

- As you present the problem (described on page 50) to students, you find three who are unable to subtract 29¢ from $1.00 accurately: they change the dollar to 99¢ to subtract. Besides simply showing them how to do the subtraction, what else can you do to help these students?

- Five students solve the problem with no difficulty at all. How can you make the problem more challenging to develop the mathematical ideas more deeply, or offer different solutions?

Once you have introduced the problem to your students, they need to make sense of what it is about for themselves. This is where Polya's first principle comes into play. Of course, you have incorporated some of the ideas as you introduced the problem. However, you also need to think about the importance of students becoming independent problem solvers. Begin with modeling and discussing the questions and answers. Students in grades 3 and up should record the answers to each question. Primary students can talk about the information as a class or in small groups. The goal here is to develop a habit of mind so that, after many experiences, these questions will be automatic to students when they are approaching a problem for the first time. At this point, you want students to explicitly answer each of the following questions.

What do I want to find out?

Begin by focusing on the question or task. Not only does it give the student a mind set on what they will be doing, but it also helps them to identify the important information in the problem and any unnecessary information. If students don't understand what it is they are trying to find out, how can they get started solving the problem?

What do I know?

Listing the pertinent information in the problem helps students to focus on important information that is connected to the question or task. Students should summarize this in their own words. Younger students can underline the important details in the problem. Older students can paraphrase and write the important information.

Do I need more information? If so, what additional information do I need?

This is a tough question for many students. It is difficult to identify what you don't know. Be prepared to support this step by modeling and asking questions that will help students to identify missing information.

There are three types of information students may need to help them solve a problem. In multi-step problems, students need to be aware that there are other questions that must be answered before they have the information to solve the problem. These problems are the most common in our mathematics classes. In some problems, students may need to use an outside source to find information before the problem can be solved. These are the types of problems we solve every day. It is important to include some problems in this category so that students do not expect all of the information they need to be in the problem itself. Using an outside source is important in all subjects and is something students should recognize. Finally, there are some problems that cannot be solved because the information needed is not available. Students should have some experience with all three types of problems.

Is there any extra information that I do not need?

A good problem should be motivating. That means it will probably include interesting information that is not necessary to reach a solution. Just as students should be able to identify the important information in the problem, eliminating extraneous information helps to hone in on the essential details.

What estimate or prediction can I make for the solution?

Asking students to make a prediction serves several purposes. First, it helps them to focus on the question being asked. Often, students will work to solve a problem and never answer the question! If they make a prediction and compare their solution to their prediction, it reminds them to be sure they answered the question. Second, making an estimate or prediction helps to build number sense and mathematical confidence. Too often, students think that the only correct answer in mathematics must be exact. Yet in many situations, an estimate will often suffice. Getting students to think about the size of an answer, the shape of a figure, or the number of possibilities will help them to see if they are in the right ballpark. This can be frustrating to students at first because they tend to focus on wanting to get the precise answer. Providing experiences with making and adjusting estimates will not only help students to see the value of estimation but will also help them to become good estimators.

Explore

In this phase, students work as a class, in small groups, with a partner, or individually to solve the problem. Students gather data, share ideas, look for patterns, make conjectures, and choose appropriate strategies. The role of the teacher is to monitor student progress by moving around the classroom and observing individual and group progress. During this phase, the teacher also asks questions to encourage student thinking. Attending to the work of each group also helps the teacher to plan the Summarize phase of the lesson by determining how to orchestrate the class discussion and sharing that will take place to conclude the lesson.

In order to be an effective facilitator of this process, consider several questions as you are planning the lesson.

Questions to Consider when Planning the Explore Phase

As you read these questions and the suggestions that follow, think about additional ideas to consider as you plan and implement the Explore phase of the lesson. Revisit these questions following your problem-solving classes. You will find you have many additional ideas as you experience and implement problem solving in your classroom!

- How will I organize the class for the Explore phase?
- What materials might students need to solve the problem?
- How will students represent and record their ideas?
- What strategies are appropriate to help students reach a solution?
- What questions can I ask to encourage more discussion and sharing among students?

- What questions can I ask to scaffold thinking if they are struggling and reaching a level of high frustration?

- What questions can I ask to help students who have reached a solution to delve more deeply into the problem?

The Explore phase is when students finalize and carry out their problem-solving plan. This begins with selecting and employing one or more of the problem-solving strategies. It is not unusual for students to select a strategy, try it out, and find it doesn't get them where they want to go. At that point, they need to rethink their approach and try another path. During the Explore phase, students move in and out of using Polya's second and third principles of *Devise and Carry Out a Plan*.

How will I organize the class for the Explore phase?

Classes may be organized so that students work individually, in pairs, as a group, or as a whole class. In your planning, you want to consider how you will pair or group students. Do you want students grouped homogeneously or heterogeneously? Be sure you use different grouping structures so that your stronger students do not feel that they are always "tutoring" those who don't get it. It is also important to not always group students by ability so groups get labeled. (Do you remember the "Robins," the "Canaries," and the "Pigeons"?) In some classes, students can pick their own groups and work together very well. In other classes, there is no way this could happen. A good teacher can recognize each type of class. Students should not always be in the same group. Allowing students to work with a variety of partners and groups brings out the best thinking in all of them.

It is important to realize that one structure is not always best. It is not unusual for Explore time to begin with having students work individually following the launch to clarify their thinking and start to plan their solution process. After a few minutes, have students come together with a partner or in a group to share their thinking. This gives each student time to have something ready to offer the group. No one gets to sit back and watch the others work. You may want to bring the class back together at some point if you see that all of the students are really struggling to get started. You may notice that there are a variety of strategies being used and may want to point that out to students so they can think about various approaches to the problem. The point here is that there is no firm recipe for how to set up the Explore part of the lesson. Student experience, difficulty of the problem, and the success of the launch all contribute to the structure of the Explore time. Flexibility is the key!

What materials might students need to solve the problem?

Think about the materials you want to have available for students to use. Will manipulatives such as tiles, linking cubes, dice, or counters be helpful? Will students need tools like calculators, rulers, or protractors? Will students need supplies such as grid paper, scissors, string, glue, markers, or chart paper? Early in problem-solving experiences, you may want to have the materials ready for students to use. However, remember that eventually you want them to be able to select the materials they need. Having a variety of materials available allows students to decide and gather those they think will be most useful to them as they work on the problem.

How will students represent and record their ideas?

There are a variety of ways students can record their problem-solving work. Remember that the process used to reach a solution is just as important as the solution itself. You want to help your students get into the habit of clearly showing and explaining the entire process they used to reach a solution. The representation of their thinking enables you to "crawl around in their head" to know and better understand what they went through to solve the problem. Encourage students to include roadblocks they met and shifts in thinking. Too often, students think that only the correct work is what is important. Valuing all of their thinking helps them to see that sometimes the best mathematical thinking and the road to a correct solution evolves from making mistakes.

A problem-solving journal is an excellent place for students to record their work. Keeping all of their solutions in one place helps to showcase their growth over time. As students increase their repertoire of problems, they will begin to recognize similar problems and want to refer back to work on a previously solved problem. This is also a place where students can reflect on their thinking, including analyzing their approach to solving a problem and how successful they were, as well as taking additional notes on strategies and ideas shared by others in the class. Many students save their problem-solving journals from year to year and treasure them. You may want to start with a template for students to use in setting up their work. There are two models included in Appendix A.

You also need to consider how students will share work during the Summarize phase of the lesson. They can share the work in their journals if you have access to a document camera. Using chart paper and markers has several advantages such as displaying student work for a period of time and encouraging class discussions around solutions. Using chart paper also allows you to revisit a solution as you continue to develop the mathematical concepts that were used in the problem.

What strategies are appropriate to help students reach a solution?

This is a loaded question! You want to have an idea of how students might approach this problem and what strategies they might use. On the other hand, except when you are introducing a strategy, it is important to allow students to choose the strategies they think will work best. Students may not select the most efficient strategies. But with practice, they will not only improve in selecting a strategy but also in combining strategies that work together. Very few rich problems are solved with a single strategy. Don't be surprised if students come up with ways to solve a problem or use strategies that never crossed your mind! It is helpful to provide a list of strategies for students to consider. This can take the form of a bulletin board display or a list that students have embedded in their journals. Becoming familiar with the vocabulary of the strategies makes them more accessible to students as they begin their problem-solving attempts.

What questions can I ask to encourage more discussion and sharing among students?

If your students have not had many opportunities to work with partners or in small groups, they may need some help getting discussions started as they begin to share ideas. Modeling this as a whole class is one way to introduce students to rich discussions. Developing group norms with the class is very helpful. As you walk around and drop in on group conversations, you also want to be ready to encourage good conversations in groups. One way to do this is to make everyone in the group responsible for the work. That means that you can ask anyone in the group a question about the work they are doing, and he or she should be able to answer. It also encourages students to help one another with the mathematical thinking that is happening in the group.

What questions can I ask to scaffold thinking if they are struggling and reaching a level of high frustration?

The answer to this question varies with the mathematics in the problem that students are solving. Remember to consider the mathematics when you first select a problem, and at the same time, how you can scaffold that mathematics when students are struggling. The questions you ask should be supportive and lead to divergent thinking rather than point to the solution process.

What questions can I ask to help students who have reached a solution to delve more deeply into the problem?

There are always students who seem to have the answer to the problem before you even finish asking it! What do you do with them? Here are a few suggestions. It is important that these students completely represent their thinking in their journals or in some other way. The answer alone does not give you the information you need to analyze and follow their thinking.

Recording the solution process enables students to think about their thinking (*metacognition*) and make connections to other mathematical ideas—both previously learned and new. It also encourages students to extend their thinking beyond the limitations of the problem.

Once the work is clearly represented, students may look for another way to solve the problem. You should be ready with a question to help them get started. For example, ask if they could solve the problem with another strategy or if they can describe and generalize the pattern they found in their solution process.

One other way to stretch student thinking is to have an extension problem ready for them to solve. It can be directly connected to the problem that the class is working on, or it can be an entirely different problem that is quite challenging.

Summarize

This part of the lesson is often overlooked, and yet it is where the main teaching occurs. It is important that ample time is reserved for summarizing the problem. Ideally, the Launch, Explore, Summarize phases should take place in one class period. However, it is also important to consider the amount of time each phase should take. Here is a good rule of thumb:

- Launch = about 10 minutes
- Explore = about 20 minutes
- Summarize = about 20 minutes

These times are not carved in stone. If students need more time to work on the problem, then the Summarize phase might have to take place on the following day. But do not skip this part of the lesson!

Once students have solved the problem, or made sufficient progress toward reaching a solution, it is time to bring them together for class discussion and sharing. Although the students do most of the talking during this phase, you need to be prepared to guide students to the important mathematical ideas and enhance their understanding of the mathematics in the problem. This is also the time that students should consider how they could refine or revise strategies they used to be effective and efficient problem-solving techniques.

The Summarize phase of the lesson incorporates the fourth of Polya's principles: *Look Back.* Students reflect on their own thinking and the thinking of others. They put together the pieces of the mathematics puzzle to make sense of the concept's meaning. This is achieved by sharing ideas, determining other solutions or strategies, making conjectures, generalizing patterns, and considering other ways to solve the problem. A great deal is happening during this part of the lesson!

Questions to Consider when Planning to Summarize

As you develop the practice of facilitating the Summarize phase of the lesson, you will have many ideas to add. Plan on revisiting these questions following your problem-solving lessons.

How will I help students make sense of the variety of methods that can be used to solve this problem?

The planning for this phase not only takes place before the lesson but also during the Explore phase. As you are working with groups and observing various approaches to the problem, you need to be thinking of which groups to have share their thinking with the entire class. Select several approaches to the problem. Begin with a workable approach that is perhaps not the most efficient, yet leads to a solution. If you start with the slickest solution, no one else in the class is going to want to share. You can think of it as building anticipation. You might even try to find two groups that have used the same strategy in two very different ways. Have both groups present and have the class talk about the differences.

How will I orchestrate the sharing and discussion of student work so that all students can reach a level of understanding of the important mathematics embedded in the problem?

As students present their work, your role is to be sure that the ideas are clear and that others in the class understand. Having students pose conjectures, ask clarifying questions, justify their reasoning, and refine their work gets everyone involved in thinking about the mathematical ideas you want to emphasize. You will need to model and encourage this type of discussion at first. The questions you ask both the presenting group and members of the class are what lead to building the mathematical understanding that should emerge from the problem.

What strategies should be shared?

It is good to have an idea of the key strategies that are effective and efficient in solving the problem. Since most problems can be solved by a variety of strategies, it is likely that you will find many approaches used by your students. So, it is important to consider whether there is a particular strategy that develops the mathematical concepts you want your students to understand. Try to decide on a good starter strategy. It may not be the most efficient, but it should be helpful to students who are struggling with the problem. It may also be helpful to find two groups that used the same strategies in very different ways. If you found a strategy that surprised you and turned out to be a very good way to solve the problem, share that as well. All of these things need to be considered as you select the groups of students who will share their thinking during this part of the lesson.

What ideas do not need to be emphasized at this time?

New ideas often come up with rich problems. There is a danger here of going off in a direction that was not your original intention. This would be a very exciting opportunity if you had an unrestricted amount of time for your mathematics lessons. However, in reality, you have limited time and specific content for your mathematics instruction. A clear focus on the goals of the lesson will help you to avoid topics and ideas that arise that are not part of the mathematics you are teaching. If students are interested in pursuing these ideas, a good classroom reference library or the Internet are wonderful places for students to explore new ideas and enrich the lesson.

What connections do I want students to make as a result of this lesson?

One of the most important aspects of planning the Summarize section in advance of the lesson is to know exactly what you want to accomplish with the problem you have selected, including the mathematical goals, the integration of the process standards, and any connections students will make from solving and discussing the problem. As you determine the mathematical goals of the lesson, you should bear in mind connections to previously learned concepts, assignments that will reinforce what students learn from solving the problem, and upcoming mathematical concepts that will be developed from this concept. This process uses the foundations of Backwards Planning and is much like concept mapping. What previous understandings and skills are needed to solve the problem? What mathematics will students take away from the problem? What future concepts and understandings will be developed from the mathematics learned from solving the problem?

Think about connections to the students' lives that might also be brought out in the Summarize section of the lesson. Connecting percents and discount prices to buying an iPod® provides a motivating example of the use and importance of mathematics in the real world and not just in mathematics class.

What will I use for follow-up practice or additional work after the lesson is complete?

Once the problem has been solved, the mathematical thinking should not end. Think about what students will need to reinforce the mathematics they have just uncovered. Do not discount the importance of practicing the skill, but select and assign practice exercises wisely. If students have explored the concepts of area and perimeter in the problem they have just solved, presenting

66

them with 20 exercises on area and perimeter serves little purpose. Having a few exercises on area and perimeter and a similar problem may be sufficient. Remember, the purposes of follow-up practice either in class or as homework is to provide some additional reinforcement for students and as an informal assessment for you to use in determining whether students understand the concepts.

Your mathematics textbook is a resource for follow-up practice and additional work. Interesting problems can be found in a variety of resources and by searching the Internet. Appendix C (pages 172–182) can help you get started.

Some Final Thoughts

The Launch, Explore, Summarize Instructional Model is a framework for planning a rich mathematics lesson. It is important to blend it to the lesson so that students move through the phases fluidly. Like any other approach, this model can become boring and obsolete if it is presented in exactly the same manner in each lesson. Think about various ways to launch the problem or task that students will complete. Group students in a variety of ways to explore the problem. Orchestrate the summary using various media including charts, the overhead projector, an interactive whiteboard, a document camera, or even the blackboard.

As you teach the lesson, you will find that you move in and out of the phases based on student needs. Some students will be ready to begin exploring during the Launch phase. In the Explore phase, you may find that you need to bring the class back together to clarify some of the students' misconceptions. As you observe students exploring, your questions should lead them to prepare for what will happen during the Summarize phase. Extension problems will have students ready to do more exploration even as they are still putting together the mathematical ideas from the lesson. As you can see, this instructional model is quite exhilarating!

Effective Questioning

An important part of helping students become effective problem solvers is to be ready with good questions. Questions that require students to think more deeply are likely to produce better learning outcomes than questions for which pupils only need to remember a fact or a routine. Too often, we tend to show students how to do something when they get stuck rather than to help them uncover the mathematics by asking the right question.

Developing good questioning skills takes purposeful practice. The following examples will help to get you started. Although these questions are organized by lesson phases, you will find that many of them can be used throughout the problem-solving lesson and as follow-up questions to encourage student reflection.

Questions to Help Launch the Problem
• Can you describe the problem in your own words?
• What do you want to find out?
• What are the important facts in the problem?
• Is there anything in the problem you do not understand?
• What questions do you still have?
• Is there anything else you need to know?
• What materials can you use to get started?
• Which strategies will you use?
• How will you record your work?

Questions to Differentiate Instruction
While Students Explore the Problem

To assess student progress, ask:

• What have you done so far?

• Explain how you are organizing your work.

• What strategies have you used? Explain how you have used them.

• Does your answer seem reasonable?

• Do you see a pattern? Can you describe the pattern?

• Have you accounted for all possibilities? How can you be sure?

• Can anyone explain it another way?

To help students who are struggling:

• Describe the problem to me in your own words.

• Are there any words you don't understand?

• What question are you trying to answer?

• What strategies have you tried so far?

• Can you make a table? Draw a picture? Act it out?

• Have you solved a similar problem?

• Can you make the numbers easier?

• Are there other materials you can use to help you?

• What ideas have we learned that may be helpful to you?

To help students identify any important information they may have overlooked, ask questions that are specific to the problem:

• Is there another step you may need to start with?

• Does your solution make sense? How can you convince me?

Questions to Differentiate Instruction While Students Explore the Problem (*cont.*)

To challenge students who have successfully solved the problem, ask:

- Will your strategy always work?

- Can you find other solutions?

- Is there another way to solve the problem?

- What would happen if . . . ?

- What patterns did you see? Can you extend the pattern for x cases?

- What if you started with a different number?

- What other problems have we solved that are like this one?

- Can you explain your work to the class?

Questions to Ask During the Summarize Phase of the Lesson

- Why did you decide to do that step? What did you learn from it?

- Do you agree with what _____ did? Why or why not?

- Did anyone get a different answer? If so, who is correct? Can you justify your reasoning?

- Did anyone solve the problem a different way? Can you describe your work?

- Who can restate what _____ just said?

- Will this method always work? Can you find a situation where it will not work?

- What did you learn from doing this problem?

Reflect and Act

Respond to the questions below in your problem-solving journal.

1. What does problem solving in the classroom look like? What does it sound like? What is the teacher doing? What are the students doing?

2. How can Polya's four-principle process help you and your students become better problem solvers?

3. What steps can you take to implement the Launch, Explore, Summarize Instructional Model in your classroom?

CHAPTER 3

Getting Started Strategies

"Students use many strategies intuitively when they solve problems. However, gaining familiarity with a collection of strategies by seeing them modeled, and then trying to apply them, provides students with useful tools for tackling problems and broadens their problem-solving abilities."

Burns 2007

Many people struggle with how to approach a problem. The strategies in this chapter can be used in a variety of settings and include the following:

- Restate the Problem in Your Own Words
- Identify Wanted, Given, and Needed information
- Identify a Subgoal
- Select Appropriate Notation

These strategies can help you to solve both routine problems as well as non-routine problems like the ones that were introduced in the previous chapter. What is important about these strategies is that they can help anyone become more comfortable with approaching a problem. Each of them will help you get started or help you to reexamine the problem if you hit a roadblock. They are often used together with the strategies we will examine in the next chapters. Time to get started on your problem-solving journey!

After initially reading a problem, it is helpful to restate the problem in your own words to be sure you understand the problem situation. Identifying wanted and given information will help you to determine any additional information needed to solve the problem.

Often, once the wanted, given, and needed information have been identified, an equation can be written to help determine what to do to solve the problem. Since multistep problems are more complicated, identifying intermediate steps required to answer the question will help you to reach a solution. Once you have an understanding of the problem situation, determining what type of notation to use—tables, drawings, diagrams, lists, or graphs—will help you to get started as well as to represent your thinking in a concrete way. Let's take a look at each of these strategies.

Unlike the problems in the next chapters, the problems in this chapter do not have grade levels assigned. The intention is to start thinking about each of these strategies as you develop your own expertise in approaching a problem. Keep in mind, however, that you should also share these strategies with your students.

Restate the Problem in Your Own Words

Understanding the Strategy

In order to solve a problem, you need to make it your own. This entails focusing on the details presented and your interpretation of that information. Part of this strategy involves focusing on the details of the problem and what it is you are trying to find out. Once you do this, you should be able to put the problem in your own words. Restating the problem without looking at the original problem is a good way to eliminate extraneous information. Many unsuccessful problem-solving attempts stem from too little time spent defining and understanding the problem.

It is not uncommon to have to read the problem several times in order to be able to restate it so that you can include all of the important information. The goal is to get to the point where you have truly focused in on the important information. A good guideline to use with students is to do three readings of the problem.

- The first reading provides a general familiarity with the information in the problem. In this stage, you begin to visualize the objects and activities in the problem. You may also begin to eliminate details of the problem that are not important to the solution process.

- The second reading helps you to put the problem into your own terminology. At this point, you begin to focus on the specifics of the problem.

- The third reading helps you reduce the problem to only the relevant ideas involved, and the problem begins to take on a workable reform.

Using the Strategy

Although these strategies vary in the level of sophistication with each grade level band, it is important to get yourself (and your students) into the habit of mind that you always need to make sense of what is happening in the problem. Too often, we rush into trying to solve the problem when we have not taken the time to comprehend what the problem is about.

Here are the steps to follow in order to restate the problem in your own words:

1. Start by visualizing the objects and activities.

2. Eliminate the unnecessary information.

3. Once you have focused on the specifics of the problem, put the problem in your own words.

4. Go back once more and record the relevant ideas of the problem.

Ready, Set, Solve

We should be striving to become good problem solvers and sharing this experience with our students. So, what other way to begin but by making sense of what we are expected to do, other than to make some sense out of the problem we are attempting to solve?

Begin to solve each of the following problems by stating the problem in your own words. Think about each of the stages you need to go through. Once you have read the problem and you are confident you know the important information, rewrite it in your journal using your own words.

A pen, a pencil, and an eraser cost $2.70 total. The pencil was $1.00 more than the eraser. The pen was $0.30 more than the pencil and eraser together. How much was the pen?

While counting her money, Beth noticed that she had the same number of dimes as nickels and the same number of quarters as nickels. How many nickels did she have if her coins were worth $2.00?

One year, one-fifth of the children in Miss Baker's class had perfect attendance records. But 28 children did not have perfect attendance records. How many children were in the class?

Identify Wanted, Given, and Needed Information

Understanding the Strategy

When you restate the problem, you should be thinking about the information that is presented in the problem. In order to focus on what information is relevant, you also need to think about what is being asked. The question or task will help you to determine which details in the problem are critical and which are unnecessary.

In some problems, you may also need some additional information. Needed information can take on different forms. One type of additional information requires that you go to an outside resource to find facts or data that may not be present in the problem. Many problems require you to take several steps, each of which provides the information you need to continue. Some problems cannot be solved because the required information is not available or is not known.

Some examples of problems that require more information are on the following page. Read each problem below and determine which of the following is true about each problem:

- The problem needs information that I can find through another source before I solve it.

- The problem needs information that requires that I do something with the facts given before I can finally get its solution.

- The problem needs information which is not known or available to me, and therefore, I cannot solve it.

> **Problem 1:** At the big holiday sale, every item at Hardware Heaven was marked down an additional 25%. The electric drill I bought was originally $68.00 and had already been marked down 15%. How much did the drill cost?

Problem 2: George Washington died on December 14, 1799. How old was he when he died?

Problem 3: How many children under the age of 12 visited the observation deck of the Empire State Building last month?

Using the Strategy

When students begin to work on problem solving, it is important to model this strategy. Be explicit by having students identify what the problem is asking, which details in the problem will help to answer that question, and what, if any, additional information is needed to solve the problem. Get students in the habit of recording wanted, needed, and given information so they will focus on looking for this information as they prepare to solve the problem. Used with the Restate the Problem strategy, this strategy will aid students in comprehending the problem as well.

It is sometimes difficult to identify needed information because it isn't explicit in the problem. Experience with problems that need additional information will help you and your students get more proficient in recognizing when more information is needed and how they will (or if they can) obtain this information. Problems in real life do not come wrapped up neatly with everything we need to solve them. Often we have to think creatively to satisfactorily reach a conclusion that will work. Mathematical problem solving should also give us the opportunity to think creatively.

Ready, Set, Solve

As you work on the following problems, first restate each in your own words. Then make a concerted effort to identify what is wanted, given, and needed for each problem. If you need more information, think about how you can get it. When you finish, go back and reread the problem. Consider these questions after rereading the problem:

- Did this strategy help to make it clearer?

- Do you have an idea of how to get started?

- Do you notice anything that you didn't notice on your first read?

When using this strategy, you can show your thinking using pictures, numbers, or words. Thinking about how you solved the problem and describing your thinking through representations and communication helps to develop a deeper understanding of the process you used to reach a solution. When we focus on the process we used to solve a problem, we can use that process to solve similar problems.

One pipe can fill a tank in three hours, and another pipe can fill the tank in six hours. How long will it take to fill the tank if both pipes are used at the same time?

Susan, her brother, her daughter, and her son all went bike riding. The fastest and slowest riders were the same age, while the slowest rider's twin was slower than the fastest. If Susan rode faster than her children, who rode the fastest?

There are 7 girls (including Ling) living on Ling's street. The average of their ages is 13. One of the girls is 16 years old, and four of the girls are two years under the average. What is Ling's age if the other girl is 13?

Identify a Subgoal

Understanding the Strategy

One of the more difficult aspects of problem solving is problems that require more than one step. Reaching an acceptable solution for some problems requires a series of steps or actions, each depending on the information gathered from the previous step or action. What makes this tricky is it may not be obvious that other steps are needed or what those steps might be. Referring back to the previous strategies of Restate the Problem in Your Own Words and Identify Wanted, Needed, and Given Information will help you to get started with breaking the problem into smaller steps in order to successfully answer the question.

Using the Strategy

This strategy is closely connected to the last part of the Identify Wanted, Needed, and Given Information strategy. If the information provided in the problem is not enough for you to get directly to a solution, you may need to complete some actions that will give you the data you need to solve the problem. These steps are not always obvious but getting started with a plan will help you to reach an approach that will provide the information.

As you introduce this strategy to students, build on the two previous strategies. Ask students questions, or better yet, give them opportunities to ask questions that will help them to identify the steps they need to take to reach a solution. It is important to have students show each step of their work clearly—using pictures, numbers, or words so that they can follow their thinking and share it with others.

Ready, Set, Solve

Take time to solve the following problems in your journal. Each of these problems requires one or more subgoals in order to reach a final solution. Think about how you are using the three strategies we have discussed. What helped you to identify the subgoals? How did they help you to reach a final solution? For both you and your students, it is important for you to show your work completely so that anyone who looks at it can understand what you did and find the answer to the question. Thinking about how you solved the problem and describing your thinking through representations and communication helps to develop a deeper understanding of the process you used to reach a solution. When we focus on the process we used to solve a problem, we can use that process to solve similar problems.

Mr. and Mrs. Jogger like to run. From past experiences they know that Mr. Jogger can run 6 km In the time it takes Mrs. Jogger to cover 4 km. They have decided that they would like to run the same distance, 9 km, and finish together. How much of a head start does Mrs. Jogger need for them to finish together?

During one school year, Stella was given 25 cents for each math test she passed and was fined 50 cents for each math test she failed. By the end of the school year, Stella passed seven times as many math tests as she failed and she had a total of $3.75. How many tests did she fail?

Use the diagram to fill in the numbers using these clues:

- Each digit 1–9 is used once.

- Row 1 is half the total of Column 1.

- Row 1 contains the prime factorization of 30.

- There are no composite numbers in Column 3.

- The sums of Column 3 and Row 2 are the same.

- Column 2 contains even and consecutive numbers.

- All corner numbers are odd and consecutive.

- There is a square number in each column.

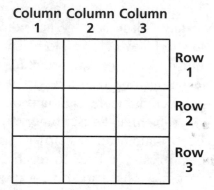

Select Appropriate Notation

Understanding the Strategy

Recall that problem solving is the first mathematical process standard in NCTM's *Principles and Standards for School Mathematics* (2000) and the first standard of mathematical practice in the Common Core Standards (2010). Problem solving is the reason we do mathematics. What is intriguing about solving problems and looking at student work is that there are many paths to a solution. Most problems require a combination of strategies and can be solved in multiple ways. The representations used in written work enable us to think more deeply about the solution as well as share our thinking with others.

The notation we use to represent our mathematical thinking can range from concrete models to pictorial representations to numerical notation to abstract symbols. The notation used to solve the problem can help to build the mathematical ideas as well as show how we solved the problem. Appropriate notation is an important aspect of the representation process standard. Interestingly, young children can solve rather complex problems using a notation that is developmentally appropriate for them and helps them to hone in on the information and actions of the problem.

Using the Strategy

Select Appropriate Notation is the culminating "getting started" strategy. You have been using a combination of these strategies to help you get started with each problem. The more experience you have with representing your thinking using appropriate notation, the more able problem solver you will become. Many of the strategies we explore in the next three chapters will also involve the notation you use to solve the problem, as well as how you use various notations to show the process that you used to reach the solution. For that reason, this strategy really has two purposes. First, you use notation to help you to reach a solution. Second, you use notation to show the process you followed to get to the solution so others can understand your thinking.

Ready, Set, Solve

The following problems can be solved in a variety of ways. As you solve each problem in your journal, think about the notation you will use to reach a solution and to show your work. An important part of a problem-solving lesson in the classroom is to give students the opportunity to share how they solved a problem. It would be more unusual to have all of the students solve a rich problem the same way than to have them come up with a variety of methods and notations. It is this divergent thinking that helps us all to become stronger problem solvers. Your challenge with this set of problems is to find more than one way to represent your thinking. If you are sharing these problems with colleagues or with students, look at how they represented their thinking. What have you learned from sharing your thinking with others?

The students at Linda's party are playing a new game. They are seated around a circular table, evenly spaced and consecutively numbered. Linda is number 5. She is directly opposite Kim who is number 16. How many students are at the party?

In this tangram puzzle, you can make many different shapes by putting the seven pieces together in different ways.

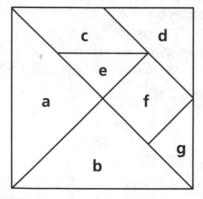

If the area of the entire puzzle is one square unit, find the area of each of the pieces.

The Wright Brothers have a collection of bicycle seats and wheels. They have a total of 26 seats and 60 wheels. They decide to make some bicycles, tricycles, and unicycles. There are more bicycles than any other type of cycles. The number of wheels they put on bicycles is close to the number of wheels they put on the tricycles. They do not use very many wheels to make the unicycles. How many of each type of cycle do they make?

Reflect and Act

Respond to the questions below in your problem-solving journal.

1. How did these problem-solving strategies help you to solve the provided problems in this chapter?

2. How will these strategies help students with comprehending the problem they are trying to solve?

3. What steps can you take to teach your students how to use these strategies when solving problems?

Getting Organized Strategies

"Most, if not all, important mathematics concepts and procedures can best be taught through problem solving. That is, tasks or problems can and should be posed that engage students in thinking about developing the important mathematics they need to learn."

NCTM 2000

In this chapter we will examine the following strategies that form the foundation for mathematical problem solving.

- Look for a Pattern
- Create a Table
- Create an Organized List
- Guess and Check

Students will begin to experience looking for a pattern within mathematical situations to develop a habit of mind to seek and build fundamental numerical relationships through identifying, extending, and generalizing patterns. The strategies of Create a Table and Create an Organized List help students to organize the information given in a problem and then apply other strategies to reach a solution. Although many students depend on Guess and Check as a means to solving a problem, through refining this strategy, students will become more efficient problem solvers.

You will find that as you become more proficient with each of the strategies, they often are used together and with other strategies to reach a solution. For example, you can organize your guesses and checks through making a list. The list will often lead to a pattern that leads to a solution much more efficiently than random guessing and checking. Read on for a closer look at these four strategies.

Look for a Pattern

Understanding the Strategy

Patterns are fundamental to mathematics. Not only is our number system based on patterns, but earlier number systems such as the Mayan, Babylonian, and Roman systems were developed from patterns. Students can learn to recognize and describe patterns as early as the primary grades. The earlier patterns become part of students' mathematical experiences the more likely they are to see the structure of mathematics and understand key concepts such as place value, operations, and geometry.

Patterns come in all forms. They can begin with objects in the environment, colors, shapes, and numbers. Students in kindergarten through grade 2 begin to identify, extend, and describe repeating patterns and then move on to growing patterns. As students enter the elementary and middle grades, the patterns become more sophisticated. Students should have many opportunities to build, extend, and describe patterns. They should also create and share their own patterns. Reasoning and communicating about patterns helps students to connect patterns to problem situations and eventually to generalize those patterns, a critical skill to success in algebra, geometry, and statistics.

Using the Strategy

This strategy is often used in combination with other strategies, including Create a Table, Create an Organized List, and Solve a Simpler Problem.

In the early grades, your goal should be for students to identify the pattern and continue with the next elements in the pattern. For example, look at the following shapes:

Identifying the rectangle shape and then two oval shapes will help the student to continue the pattern by adding another rectangle and two ovals.

Extending this to a number situation, students in the early grades should be able to identify the pattern for the following sequence:

$$0, 2, 4, 6, 8, \_\_\_\_$$

Note that these numbers differ by 2, or you add 2 to the current number to get the next number, or that the numbers are the even numbers. All of these are acceptable descriptions of the pattern. By applying one of the "rules," you can continue the sequence.

In the elementary and middle grades, the patterns become more complex. Look at this pattern:

$$3, 7, 12, 18, \_\_\_\_$$

In this case we are adding consecutive numbers to each number to get the next number in the sequence: $3 + 4 = 7$; $7 + 5 = 12$; $12 + 6 = 18$. What is the next number in the sequence?

In the problems that follow, pay close attention to the use of patterns. How can you encourage students to look for patterns in the work they do in mathematics? Students' experiences with patterns should be an integral part of the curriculum at every grade level.

Ready, Set, Solve

Use the Look for a Pattern strategy to solve these problems. Take time to record your work in your journal. Make a note of any patterns you find as you solve the problem, not as a passive observation but so that you can work to extend those patterns for a given situation. The ultimate goal is to generalize the pattern to fit any situation. Show your thinking using pictures, numbers, or words. Thinking about how you solved the problem and describing your thinking through representations and writing helps to develop a deeper understanding of your process. When you focus on the process you used to solve a problem, you can use that process to solve similar problems.

Grades K–2

Marta is reading a book for her summer reading club. On the first day, she read two pages. On the second day, she read five pages. On the third day, she read eight pages. How many pages did Marta read on the sixth day?

Grades 3–5

For recess time, our class would like one minute on the first day of school, two minutes on the second day, four minutes on the third day, eight minutes on the fourth day, and so on. If our teacher accepts the plan, how long will recess be at the end of the second week of school? Express your answer in more than one way.

Grades 6–8

Larry is having a party. The first time the doorbell rings, one person enters. Each time the doorbell rings, a group enters that contains two more than the previous group. What is the total number of guests at the party after the doorbell rings 10 times?

Create a Table

Understanding the Strategy

One way to help organize the information in a problem is to create a table. Once the information is organized in a table, students can look for relationships and extend the table to help solve the problem. A table can be very helpful when used together with the Find a Pattern or Guess and Check strategies. Tables not only help students to organize data but also can assist them in recognizing connections in the problem and communicating their thinking about those connections.

Using the Strategy

In the early grades, teachers should model the Create a Table strategy. Both vertical and horizontal table layouts should be used. However, when one of the layouts is introduced, stay with that type until students are comfortable with it. Label each column or row in the table to help students know what information goes in each column or row. When first using tables, the order of the items is not critical. As students feel comfortable with making tables, organizing the information should become part of the process. This helps students to find patterns and to see if they have all possible solutions.

By grade 3, students should begin to make their own tables with little help from the teacher. If students have not had any previous experience with creating tables, spend some time modeling and talking about the process of creating a table before expecting students to do it independently. In grades 3–5, creating tables should become an important part of organizing ideas throughout mathematics class and in other subjects as well.

With adequate experience in the elementary grades, middle school students should continue to create tables. This is also a good time to think about connections to algebraic concepts, including graphing and making generalizations.

Here are two examples of tables that your students might use. As students are beginning to work with tables, you may want to help them to determine the headings. Remember that you should stick with one type of table until students are comfortable with it. Once students become proficient with using tables, they should begin constructing their tables independently.

How many wheels on eight tricycles?

Tricycles	Wheels
1	3
2	6
3	9
4	12
5	15
6	18
7	21
8	24

They say that each year of a human's life is equivalent to seven years in a dog's life. If Fido has lived four human years, what is his life in dog years?

Human Years	1	2	3	4
Dog Years	7	14	21	28

One kilometer (km) is about 0.62 of a mile. The speed limit in Canada is 100 km per hour. How fast is that in miles per hour?

Km per hour	10	20	30	40	50	60	70	80	90	100
Miles per hour	6.2	12.4	18.6	24.8	31	37.2	43.4	49.6	55.8	62

Ready, Set, Solve

Take time to solve the problems that follow in your journal. Remember to think about using the strategy of creating a table. Think about how you will set up a table to organize the information you have been given and the information you will need to find. Also think about how the table helps you to recognize and extend a pattern. Reflect on how the table helps you to reach a solution and determine if other solutions may be possible. Be sure to answer the question in the problem. Once you have solved the problem, think about how the table helped you to organize your work. Reflecting on how you solved the problem and describing your thinking through representations and communication helps to develop a deeper understanding of the process you used to reach a solution. When we focus on the process we used to solve a problem, we can use that process to solve similar problems.

The more experience you and your students have with situations that require a table, the better you will get at setting up tables to organize you work and your thinking.

Grades K–2

Jonathan wants to buy a candy bar that costs a quarter. He has pennies, nickels, and dimes, but no quarters in his pocket. How can he pay for the candy bar with exactly 25¢?

Grades 3–5

Suzanne and Jose work at the city garden in the summer. Suzanne comes every third day to water all of the plants. Jose comes every fifth day to pull weeds. They never miss a day—even on weekends! If they are both working at the garden today, how many times will they be working on the same day in the next 6 weeks?

Grades 6–8

Iggy loves ice cream! His favorite flavor is caramel pecan swirl. His little sister, Izzy also loves ice cream. In fact, she loves every flavor! Last week Iggy put a gallon of ice cream in the freezer. That night, Izzy ate half of the ice cream. The next night she ate half of what was left. This continued for a total of six nights. On the seventh day, Iggy decided to have some of his ice cream. Boy, was he surprised when he opened the container! How much ice cream was left for Iggy? How much ice cream did Izzy eat?

Create an Organized List

Understanding the Strategy

Making an organized list involves keeping track of possible combinations and solutions in a systematic way. Once the possibilities are listed, if any do not fit the conditions of the problem, they can be eliminated.

There are different types of lists you can make in solving problems. Some examples include tree diagrams, charts, and matrices. Creating an organized list is helpful because it helps students review what they have already done and identify other steps that may be needed to solve the problem.

Here is a sample problem that utilizes a tree diagram:

Marco has 3 shirts, 2 pairs of pants, and 2 different pairs of shoes. How many different outfits can he wear?

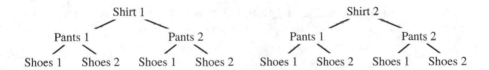

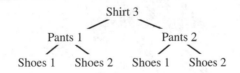

Here is a sample problem that utilizes a chart:

Harry can never remember the combination to his locker. However, he does remember these clues:

The number is 3 digits.

The digit in the tens place is greater than 6.

The digit in the ones place is even.

The digit in the hundreds place is less than 4.

The number can be evenly divided by 4.

What could Harry's locker number be?

174	274	374
184	**284**	**384**
194	294	394

The only numbers on the list that are evenly divisible by 4 are 184, 284 and 384, so one of them must be Harry's locker number!

Here is a sample problem that utilizes a matrix:

> Students Al Johnson, Bill Kilson, and Cathy Lamay were born in Michigan, Nevada, and Ohio, but not necessarily in that order. Each has a different type of pet.
>
> - Bill Kilson hates dogs.
>
> - The student with the hamster was born in Nevada.
>
> - Al Johnson's cat scratched the dog that belongs to the person from Ohio.
>
> Who is from Michigan?

	Michigan	Nevada	Ohio	dog	cat	hamster
Al Johnson	✓	✗	✗	✗	✓	✗
Bill Kilson	✗	✓	✗	✗	✗	✓
Cathy Lamay	✗	✗	✓	✓	✗	✗

Using the Strategy

When you are ready to introduce this strategy with your students, work together with the class, asking for student input, to model how to organize information. This will help students to develop ways to organize their data or solutions. There are often several ways to organize a list of information, so it is important to let students work on their own and share their lists with the rest of the class once they have the idea.

One type of problem that can be efficiently approached with an organized list is a problem that requires you to find all of the possible combinations. Practice with these types of problems will help problem solvers gain skill in organizing their work and seeing patterns. Questions to consider include:

- How did you organize the information in your list?

- Did anyone organize the information in a different way?

- How do you know you have found all of the possibilities?

- Did you recognize a pattern that can be extended?

It is also important to help students consider how they can keep information organized in a way that ensures that they have not repeated possibilities and that they have exhausted all of the options in reaching a solution. Don't worry about this at the beginning. Once students become comfortable with making a list, they can begin to analyze how to organize their work so they do not miss or repeat a possible answer.

Ready, Set, Solve

Take time to solve the following problems in your journal. Consider using the strategy of making an organized list. Think about how the list helps you to gather the possible solutions and determine which fit the conditions of the problem. Remember to answer the question that is asked in the problem. Thinking about how you solved the problem and describing your thinking through representations and communication helps to develop a deeper understanding of the process you used to reach a solution. When we focus on the process we used to solve a problem, we can use that process to solve similar problems.

Grades K–2

How many different ways can you make 10 using addition and using three addends?

(**Note:** The order of the numbers doesn't matter: 3 + 3 + 4 is the same as 4 + 3 + 3)

Grades 3–5

Mark and Sara love pizza. They both like the following toppings on their pizza:

- pepperoni
- chicken
- sausage
- pineapple
- mushrooms
- extra cheese

They want to order a pizza to share, but they only have enough money for three toppings. How many different combinations are possible?

Grades 6–8

Pat has a new bicycle lock. It's the kind that has a four-number combination. If the combination has four different numbers between 1 and 9 and all the numbers in the combination are even numbers, how many possible combinations would there be for Pat's lock?

Guess and Check

Understanding the Strategy

One of the most frequently discounted strategies is Guess and Check. Guessing the solution of a problem is sometimes associated with wild guessing. An important part of this strategy is making an educated guess based on careful attention to the important aspects of the problem. The key element in this strategy is the checking process in which the student makes an educated guess and then checks it against the problem conditions to improve his or her next guess. The student repeats this process until he or she has an acceptable answer. Students who can use guess and check efficiently often have excellent reasoning ability and do not need to wait to learn abstract processes to solve a problem.

Using the Strategy

Using estimation will help you and your students to hone in on a reasonable guess with which to begin. Sometimes we are uncomfortable with making an estimate or guess because we have been taught that in mathematics, we should follow a particular rule or algorithm. Guess and Check can be used with the Make a Table strategy to keep track of each guess as well as to see how close it is to the conditions presented in the problem. Keeping track of the guesses and checks will help you and your students to adjust each guess to get closer until the solution is reached.

Here is an example of a problem that can be efficiently solved using the Guess and Check strategy. Note how each guess helps to get closer to the actual solution.

In the art classroom the tables each have four legs and the stools each have three legs. If there are 68 legs altogether, how many tables and how many stools are there?

Guess	1	2	3
Tables	3	4	5
Stools	10	10	16
Total Legs	12 + 30 = 42	16 + 30 = 46	20 + 48 = 68

After the second guess, the solver realizes that four tables would have 16 legs and that leaves an additional 52 legs. Since 52 cannot be divided evenly by 3, there cannot be four tables. So she guesses five tables. Five tables would have 20 legs, and that leaves 48 legs. Sixteen stools with three legs each would give a total of 48 legs, so that must be the correct answer. This solution shows the efficient use of Guess and Check to reach a solution.

Ready, Set, Solve

Take time to solve the following problems in your journal. Consider using the strategy of Guess and Check. After each check, think about how you can adjust the next guess to fit the conditions in the problem. How might you use a table to help keep track of your guesses and checks? How does the table help you to revise your guess to get closer to the solution? Thinking about how you solved the problem and describing your thinking through representations and communication helps to develop a deeper understanding of the process you used to reach the solution. When we focus on the process we used to solve a problem, we can use that process to solve similar problems.

Grades K–2

When Matty emptied his piggy bank, he had nine coins, including pennies, nickels, and dimes. When he counted the value of the coins, he had 58¢. What coins did Matty have in his bank?

Grades 3–5

The animal shelter has 10 more cats than dogs. They found homes for two cats and took in two dogs. Now there are twice as many cats as dogs. How many cats does the animal shelter have now?

Grades 6–8

You have probably heard the tale of Ali Baba and the 40 thieves. I'll bet you never heard the story about his brother Bubba. One night, Bubba followed Ali and watched him enter the cave where they had hidden the stolen fortune. Later, Bubba returned to the cave and spoke the magic words *Open Sesame*. The cave opened, and Bubba went inside. He was amazed to find 2,290 pounds of rubies and emeralds. There were four times as many 1-pound rubies as 3-pound rubies. He found three times as many 3-pound emeralds as 6-pound emeralds. How many rubies and how many emeralds of each size did Bubba Baba find in the cave?

Reflect and Act

Respond to the questions below in your problem-solving journal.

1. Which strategy did you find the most useful? Why?

2. Which strategy did you struggle with the most? Why?

3. Think about how you will use these strategies with your students. What do you want to be sure to include as students become familiar with these strategies?

4. Find a problem you can use with your students that would use one of these strategies. Record it in your journal. How will you introduce the problem to your students?

CHAPTER 5

Visualizing Strategies

"We believe that if we want students to understand mathematics, it is more helpful to think of understanding as something that results from solving problems, rather than something we can teach directly."

Heibert et al. 1997

In this chapter, we will explore four strategies that help the problem solver to visualize what is happening in a problem. They are:

- Make a Model
- Draw a Picture or Diagram
- Act It Out
- Make or Use a Graph

All of these strategies require you to get involved with the problem in ways that require more than simply writing the information or using an algorithm to solve the problem. The Make a Model strategy encourages the use of manipulatives. Draw a Picture or Diagram will help to make a visual representation of the problem. With some problems, acting out the situation (Act It Out) helps make sense of the information presented. Making a graph such as a bar graph, line plot, or Venn diagram enables you to collect or organize data to answer a specific question or to draw conclusions about the data.

As you read the descriptions of each strategy and solve the problems, the strategies from Chapter 2 will help to organize your work and draw conclusions. A combination of strategies will help you to reach a solution efficiently and with an understanding of a process that can be used to solve a variety of problems.

Make a Model

Understanding the Strategy

Using a model to solve a problem offers several advantages. By visualizing the elements in the problem, you can focus on the relevant information and ignore the unessential details. In other words, it helps you to simplify and make sense out of the problem situation by using concrete materials. You can move the objects around as you change your thinking throughout the problem-solving process. This can become quite cumbersome if you are trying to solve these problems with paper and pencil.

While the main focus of this strategy is to be able to manipulate the materials, it is often used with the recording strategies you learned in Chapter 2. Creating a table or organized list can help you to keep track of your work so that you have a way to record the steps you are taking to solve the problem. It is not unusual to also Find a Pattern as you Make a Model. This will enable you to hone in on the path to a solution without having to try every possibility. This strategy is also very useful when used with Guess and Check because it helps you to see relationships and refine your guesses until you reach a successful solution.

Using the Strategy

As you solve the following problems, keep in mind the following steps:

1. Decide which materials can be used to model the information in the problem. You can use manipulatives such as square tiles, linking cubes, measuring tools, coins, or toothpicks to represent the materials in the problem.

2. Determine how to get started. Ask yourself what information is given in the problem and how you can use the materials to model that information.

3. Think about how you will document your work so that you have a written record of your solution process. This is important for going back to review what you did to solve the problem when you want to share your solution with someone else or when you come upon a similar problem that can be solved using the same or a similar process.

Here is a good example of a problem for which the Make a Model strategy would be useful. Get some coins and try it!

Look at the triangle below. Move exactly three pennies so that the triangle points down.

Respond to the questions below in your problem-solving journal.

- Why is Make a Model a good strategy for this penny problem?

- What materials could you use to represent the information if you do not have pennies?

- How can you keep track of your work so that once the problem is solved, you have access to your solution process?

Ready, Set, Solve

Take time to solve these problems in your journal. Use the Make a Model strategy. Think about the materials you can use for your model. Think about how you will represent the information in the problem with the materials you have selected. Be sure to document your solution process so that you can review or share your work with others. Using pictures, numbers, or words will help you to record your work. Thinking about how you solved the problem and describing your thinking through representations and communication helps to develop a deeper understanding of the process you used. When we focus on the process we used to solve a problem, we can use that process to solve similar problems.

Grades K–2

Tonight's dinner includes peas and carrots. You HATE peas and carrots! Rather than eat them, you count them. You have 12 vegetables on your plate. How many peas could you have? How many carrots could you have?

Grades 3–5

How many ways can five squares be arranged so that each square only touches a full side?

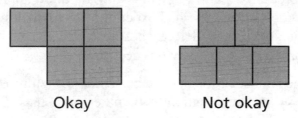

Okay   Not okay

Be careful of shapes that are rotations or reflections of pieces you have already found.

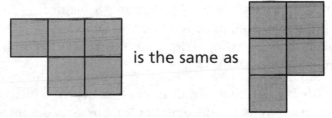

is the same as

Grades 6–8

You want to make a container to hold some pebbles you have collected on the beach. All you have is a piece of cardboard that is 8" × 11". You decide to roll it into a cylinder. You can roll it horizontally, which is 11" tall, or vertically, which is 8" tall. If you want your container to hold the maximum amount of pebbles, which way should you roll the cardboard?

Draw a Picture or Diagram

Understanding the Strategy

When students get stuck on a problem, we often suggest they draw a picture to show what they know. Drawing a picture or diagram is a way to represent the information in the problem visually. "Seeing" the information and actions in a problem helps you to understand or clarify the facts so that you can begin to decide steps to take to reach a solution. Keep in mind that drawing a picture is a more abstract representation of the information than making a model, and therefore, this is a strategy that may be more appropriate for use with students who have had experiences with making a model. In some situations, a model can be more efficient than a picture (e.g., the problems in the previous section).

As with the Make a Model strategy, Draw a Picture or Diagram is often used in combination with other strategies. While the drawing provides a pictorial representation of the problem, it may be necessary to create a table or list to keep track of your numerical thinking. Some students prefer to begin with a model and keep track of their work by drawing a picture. Others may start with a model and, once they have a deeper understanding of the problem, move to using a drawing or diagram to continue with their solution process.

Students often ask about the difference between a picture and a diagram. A *picture* is a representation that depicts the information in the problem. A *diagram* can be a more abstract representation of the problem. Consider these problems:

> Each evening, Larry takes his dog, Archie, for a walk. Archie is a very large dog. Every time they pass five houses, Archie turns around and pulls Larry back two houses. Then Larry pulls Archie forward five houses, and—you guessed it—Archie pulls Larry back two houses. If they need to walk past 20 houses in order to make it around the block and back to Larry's house, how many times will Larry have to pull Archie forward?

A 12-inch board was cut into two pieces so that the shorter piece was half as long as the larger piece. How long was the short piece?

Using the Strategy

Recall Polya's principles from Chapter 2. In order to represent a problem with a picture or diagram, it is important to begin with the information given in the problem and follow the steps below.

1. Identify the key information that is critical to the solution.

2. Eliminate details that embellish the problem but can be ignored when you are actually solving the problem.

3. Determine how you will represent the information that you will use.

Remember, if one way to draw the picture or diagram isn't working, it is okay to change your representation. With some problems you may want to use drawings to show each step of your solution. In other cases, the drawing may be enough to get you started, and you can move to a more abstract representation using numbers or an algorithm.

Ready, Set, Solve

Take time to solve the following problems in your journal. Use the strategy of Draw a Picture or Diagram. How does your drawing help you to represent the information in the problem? How can you use the drawing to help translate the information in the problem into numbers or words? Be sure to answer the question in the problem. Thinking about how you solved the problem and how describing your thinking through representations and communication helps to develop a deeper understanding of the process you used to reach a solution. When we focus on the process we used to solve a problem, we can use that process to solve similar problems.

Grades K–2

Azziza invited 6 friends to her birthday party. Each person at the party received a cup with 5 chocolate candies and 2 sticks of gum. How many chocolate candies and how many sticks of gum were given at the party?

Grades 3–5

Ellen has season tickets to the ballpark. Her seat is in section 22. The row is second from the front and eighth from the back. Each row seats 15 people. How many seats are in section 22?

Grades 6–8

Larry and Linda want to build a garden that will be placed right next to the garage. They have 100 yards of fencing to put around the garden to keep out the rabbits. They would like to make the largest rectangular garden possible. All of the sides must be whole numbers. Determine the best size for the garden.

Act It Out

Understanding the Strategy

Act It Out is a strategy that is similar to Make a Model and Draw a Picture in that it helps students visualize what is happening in the problem. Often this strategy is used together with Make a Model, because with manipulatives or concrete materials can help you act out the problem. Sometimes it is difficult to determine the first action step to take in a problem, so physically representing the problem helps to clarify your thinking and understanding. Going through the motions of the problem makes it easier to discover relationships that will lead to a solution.

This strategy can be employed by students of all ages. Young students will need practice identifying the important information in the problem and will enjoy role-playing to find the solution. Middle-grade students will find that this strategy may provide entry into a problem that does not lend itself to any of the other strategies.

Using the Strategy

In order to act out a problem, you need to understand the situation being presented. In other words, you are defining the story that is taking place. Determine any materials that are needed to help you act it out. Since this strategy may involve more than one person, the problem solvers need to think about how they are going to proceed and how to record the actions. It is helpful to have one person take the role of narrator (or director) to oversee the process and another person to be the recorder and document the work.

It is critical to understand the problem and consider all of the information as you determine how you will act it out. It is not unusual to notice details that may have been overlooked as you go through the role-playing process. There is nothing wrong with starting again and considering the additional details. This also speaks for the importance of reviewing a solution in terms of the original problem or conditions so that no details are overlooked that might have an implication for the accuracy of the solution.

As with the other strategies in this chapter, the Act It Out strategy should be used in conjunction with other strategies so that students can communicate their thinking and the process used to reach a solution. They might decide to describe the process they used to act it out. They can develop a list or table to record what is happening as they complete the problem. It is not unusual for patterns to arise as students are acting out the problem, and therefore they can draw conclusions and solve the problem using numbers, especially with more complicated situations.

Ready, Set, Solve

Take time to solve the following problems in your journal. Gather some colleagues and have some fun with acting out each of these problems. Even if you can solve it using another strategy, acting it out will give you a better sense of what your students go through when they use this strategy to solve problems. You may also be surprised by the solutions you find when you act it out. Are they different from the result you would have achieved if you had solved it with paper and pencil? Are they more efficient? Do they lead you to think about the problem in other ways? How will you communicate your solution process? Thinking about how you solved the problem and describing your thinking through representations and communication helps to develop a deeper understanding of the process you used to reach a solution. When we focus on the process we used to solve a problem, we can use that process to solve similar problems.

Grades K–2

Marcy puts coins in her piggy bank every week. There is a total of 50¢ in the bank. What coins could she have if there are six coins in the bank? Seven coins? Eight coins?

Grades 3–5

Darren bought a bike for $50. Later that summer, he sold it to his friend Dennis for $60. He bought it back for $70 and then sold it for $80. Did he earn or lose money, and if so, how much? Or, did he come out even?

Grades 6–8

You are having a birthday party. When the first person arrives, you shake her hand. As each new guest arrives, he or she shakes hands with everyone at the party. There is a total of 10 people at the party. If each person shakes hands with everyone else exactly one time, how many handshakes will there be?

Make or Use a Graph

Understanding the Strategy

Creating a graph is commonly used to solve real world problems. In using this strategy, students should have experience in each of the following scenarios:

- Questions are posed in a problem context.

- Questions are posed by the teacher.

- Questions are generated by students themselves.

Dealing with data can also happen in a variety of contexts:

- Students collect and organize data in an appropriate graph and draw conclusions.

- A graph is provided in the context of the problem, and students use the graphical representation to make inferences and draw conclusions.

There are many ways to organize data. Bar graphs, circle graphs, line graphs, and pictographs are among the most common ways; however, scatter plots and stem-and-leaf plots are also useful. A Venn diagram is a way to help represent data that may be related and overlap. The Venn diagram is made up of two or three overlapping circles. Each circle describes one characteristic of the data. The overlapping area of the circles includes data that has more than one characteristic. Consider this problem:

The 30 fifth-graders at Euclid Elementary School are planning their class party. They have taken a survey regarding favorite pizza toppings. In the class, 17 students like pepperoni on their pizzas, and 21 like mushrooms. There are two vegetarians in the class who will only eat cheese. Of all the students, how many want both pepperoni and mushroom on their pizza? Use a Venn diagram to help solve the problem.

Using the Strategy

There are a variety of ways this strategy can be used. In some situations, a graph will be provided and the students must interpret the data and make inferences to answer the question. In other situations, data will be provided and students must determine how to best organize the data to solve the problem. Perhaps the best place to start is to pose a question (or have students pose a question) and collect the data to answer the question. Remember that giving students many experiences to organize and interpret data will help them to use data in a variety of situations outside the mathematics classroom. Organizing, graphing, and interpreting data is a critical skill in science. Looking at data provided in the media and drawing conclusions about that data is an important life skill.

Keep in mind the appropriateness of graph types as you consider the age level and experience of the students with whom you are working. Young children should have experience with real graphs, picture graphs, tallies, frequency tables, and bar graphs. Upper-elementary students can begin to work with histograms, line plots, Venn diagrams, and circle graphs. Middle school students who have had experience with a variety of graphical representations can begin to work with double-bar graphs, box-and-whisker plots, and scatter plots. All of these representations will help students to become quantitatively literate as they deal with data.

Ready, Set, Solve

Take time to solve the following problems in your journal. These problems are designed for you to represent data in a format that will help you to answer the question. The representation of the data is an important part of the solution process and is part of the solution. Consider how the representation you chose supports your conclusions and leads to the solution. Think about how the graph helps you to organize the information and leads to drawing a conclusion that will satisfy the problem. How you can adapt these problems to use with students? Your awareness of how you solved the problem and the act of describing your thinking through representations and communication will help you develop a deeper understanding of your own thought processes as you reached the solution. Focusing on the process we used to solve a problem helps us to apply that process to other similar problems.

Grades K–2

The second-graders are playing a dice game. They roll 2 dice, add the numbers, and move that number of spaces on the game board. Fred is wondering which sum comes up the most often when you roll two dice. So, the students decide to collect some data to find out. Roll two dice 50 times and use a graph to keep track of the rolls. How would you answer Fred's question?

Grades 3–5

The new Bouncy Ball is quite special. Each time the ball bounces, it bounces half as high as the time before. The ball Is dropped from a tower that is 128 feet tall. It is caught when it bounces up one foot. How many times did the ball hit the ground before it was caught?

Grades 6–8

The Lincoln Middle School Basketball team has 14 players. They are listed at three positions: forward, center, and guard. When the manager counts the centers and guards, she counts eight players. When she counts the forwards and the centers, she counts nine players. How many centers, how many forwards, and how many guards are on the team?

Reflect and Act

Respond to the questions below in your
problem-solving journal.

1. Which strategy was most difficult for you? Why?
   How can you become more comfortable with using
   this strategy?

2. Were any of these strategies new to you? If so,
   how did they help you think about solving problems
   in a different way?

3. Which strategy do you think you will use with
   your students first? Use one of the resources
   mentioned to find a problem to use to model the
   strategy with your students.

Advanced Thinking Strategies

"Teachers can help and guide their students, but understanding occurs as a by-product of solving problems and reflecting on the thinking that went into those problem solutions."

Lester 2003

In this chapter, we will look at strategies that help you to approach a problem in another way. The strategies presented in this chapter are as follows:

- Solve a Simpler Problem
- Account for All Possibilities
- Work Backwards
- Change Your Point of View

Solve a Simpler Problem helps to make the problem more manageable. In real-life problems, there is often more than one solution. Account for All Possibilities helps you to ensure that you have considered all of the reasonable answers that fit the conditions of the problem. In some problems, you may know the final outcome and want to find the situation at the beginning of the problem. In this case, Work Backwards is a very helpful strategy. When you are really stumped by a problem, it is often helpful to start all over with a different point of view.

These strategies require more sophisticated thinking than the strategies we have explored in previous chapters. Although students in kindergarten through grade 3 can certainly have some early experiences with each of these, keep the problems very simple and save a formal introduction to these strategies for students in grades 4 and 5.

Solve a Simpler Problem

Understanding the Strategy

When faced with a complex problem, making it simpler will help you to get started. Simplifying a problem involves changing the problem so that it becomes understandable. This allows for a solution method to become apparent and can often be generalized by finding a pattern. This strategy is not only helpful for solving problems but can also help students to see relationships in mathematical situations rather than memorizing procedures and rules.

Using the Strategy

There are many ways to simplify a problem. Each is used in a different situation and involves a different level of complexity. Here are two ways to simplify a problem:

1. Using simpler numbers to solve a problem can help you to recognize the setting of the problem and identify the operation to use. This is a good strategy for young children, especially when they are using problems to develop conceptual understanding of number and operations. For example, a problem may present a situation in which students can use repeated addition in place of multiplication. This type of problem is often presented in mathematics textbooks.

2. The less-familiar approach involves beginning with a simpler case of the problem and building with successive cases that will lead to a solution. In the process of solving the problem, a pattern may be discovered that can be generalized for any number of cases. This strategy is often used with other strategies such as Create a Table, Draw a Diagram, or Create an Organized List in order to record the result of working through successive cases. Once the table is constructed, identifying the pattern enables you to continue to solve the problem by applying the pattern to each successive case.

Think how you can simplify the problems below to help you get started. Notice that the original problem is quite difficult to tackle, yet starting with a simpler situation makes the problem much more approachable.

Find the sum of the first 50 odd numbers.

Simplify: Begin by finding the sum of the first two odd numbers.

$$1 + 3 = 4$$

Move on to the first three odd numbers, then to the first four odd numbers.

$$1 + 3 + 5 = 9$$

$$1 + 3 + 5 + 7 = 16$$

Keep track of your work in a table and continue until you notice a pattern. Once you notice a pattern, you can continue to increase the number of addends, or if you can generalize the pattern, you can jump to 50 addends. In fact, you can then solve this problem for any number of addends!

A football team of 12 players must choose a captain and a co-captain. How many different combinations are possible?

Simplify: How many combinations would be possible for a team with three players? four players?

Making a tree diagram will help to keep track of the possibilities. Can you find the pattern? Can you determine the answer to this problem by extending the pattern?

Three players   (A, B, C)

Captain   Co-captain

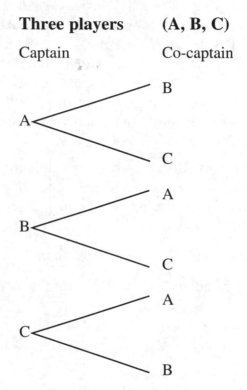

With three players there are six possibilities.

Four players   **(A, B, C, D)**

Captain   Co-captain

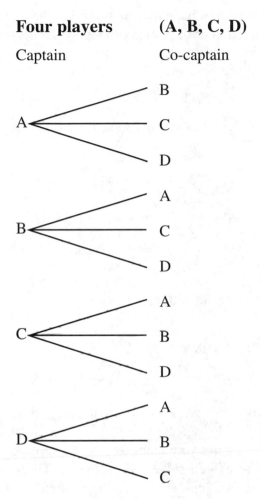

With four players there are 12 possibilities.

Continue the tree diagrams until you think you have the pattern and can identify the number of combinations for 12 players.

Find the product:

$$5^5 \times 5^8$$

Start with a simpler situation and look for a pattern.

$$5^1 \times 5^1 = 5 \times 5 = 5^2$$

$$5^1 \times 5^2 = 5 \times 5 \times 5 = 5^3$$

$$5^2 \times 5^2 = 5 \times 5 \times 5 \times 5 = 5^4$$

$$5^2 \times 5^3 = 5 \times 5 \times 5 \times 5 \times 5 = 5^5$$

Continue with additional examples until you find the pattern. Can you generalize a rule for multiplying any numbers with exponents?

Ready, Set, Solve

Solve these problems by solving a simpler problem. Begin by thinking about how you can simplify the situation in the problem. As you record your work in your journal, think about other strategies that will help you to organize your results. Show your thinking using pictures, numbers, or words. Make a note of any patterns you find as you solve the problem. Thinking about how you solved the problem and describing your thinking through representations and communication helps to develop a deeper understanding of the process you used to reach a solution. When we focus on the process we used to solve a problem, we can use that process to solve similar problems.

Grades K–2

Miranda loves to count. On her way to school today, she counted these things:

- One white kitten sitting on the front porch.
- Two frogs hopping across the street.
- Three robins singing in the tree.
- Four grasshoppers jumping along the sidewalk.
- Five poodles going for a walk.
- Six squirrels climbing up the trees.
- Seven fire hydrants painted red.
- Eight daffodils swaying in the wind.
- Nine pine trees with pine cones hanging low.
- Ten acorns sitting on the ground.

How many things did Miranda count altogether?

Grades 3–5

Tony's restaurant has 30 small tables to be used for a banquet. Each table can seat only one person on each side. If the tables are pushed together to make one long table, how many people can sit at the table?

Grades 6–8

How many squares of any size are on a standard 8 × 8 chessboard?

Account for All Possibilities

Understanding the Strategy

Too often we reach a solution to a problem without realizing there are other possible answers. In our everyday life, there are very few problems we encounter that have only one solution (although there may be a best solution). Accounting for all possibilities helps you to determine not only whether you have found all of the answers that fit the problem but also whether you have eliminated all the solutions that do not work. A key part of this strategy is to *systematically* account for all possibilities. This means that you do not have to examine all of the potential possibilities but rather that each possibility must be accounted for. In other words, through your work, you can eliminate possibilities that do not fit the condition of the problem.

Using the Strategy

As with many of the previous strategies we have examined, it is helpful to use Account for All Possibilities in conjunction with other strategies. To get started with this strategy, it might be helpful to set up a table or organized list. The critical link here is that your work should be organized. This means that once you find a solution that fits the conditions of the problem, you need to consider additional solutions that also fit. Through an organized approach, you will not waste time with incorrect solutions because you can eliminate them through reasoning. You could consider this strategy an extension of making an organized list because there is more reasoning involved with considering whether you have found all of the possible solutions. You may find that you begin with Guess and Check. As you eliminate incorrect solutions, you can hone in on the characteristics of solutions that work.

Let's look at some ways to organize your thinking that will help to Account for All Possibilities. Study the following problems and solutions. What do you notice about how the work is represented?

Notice that not all possible combinations have been tried. As you work through the problems, you can reason which trials can be eliminated. How can you be sure that all of the possible solutions have been accounted for?

> Francine went to the store to buy some fruit. She can get three oranges for 50¢. She has lots of coins but no half-dollars and no pennies. Find all of the combinations of coins she could use to pay for the oranges. One way to pay is with two quarters. Find the other combinations. How do you know you have all of them?

> There are some very strange creatures on the planet Mathoid. Some creatures have two eyes and some have three eyes. On my last visit, I counted a total of 23 eyes. How many of each creature did I meet on Mathoid?

> Mark and his father are putting up a fence in their backyard. Some sections are 15 feet long and the others are 18 feet long. What is the least number of sections they can put up so that the fence is 270 feet long? How many of each will they use?

Ready, Set, Solve

Take time to solve the following problems in your journal. Remember to think about using the strategy of Account for All Possibilities. Also consider using a table. Think about how the table helps you to recognize and extend a pattern. Be sure to answer the question in the problem. How does the table help you to organize your work? Thinking about how you solved the problem and describing your thinking through representations and communication helps to develop a deeper understanding of the process you used to reach a solution. When we focus on the process we used to solve a problem, we can use that process to solve similar problems.

Grades 1–3

Rachelle's house number has three different digits.

The sum of the three digits is 12.

The number is greater than 480.

What could the house number be?

Do you think you found all the possible solutions?

Grades 3–5

Mrs. Fairweather has placed 12 tiles in a bag. Some are red, some are blue, and some are yellow. There are no other colors. How many different combinations of tiles are possible?

Grades 6–8

Mutt and Jeff are playing a game with the spinner shown here. They spin twice and add the fractions. If the sum is greater than $\frac{1}{2}$, Jeff gets a point. If the sum is less than $\frac{1}{2}$, Mutt gets a point. Is the game fair? Explain your reasoning.

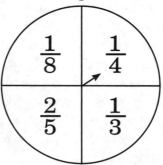

Work Backwards

Understanding the Strategy

Problems in which the final outcome is presented and the question asks about the original situation are best solved using the Work Backwards strategy. What is interesting about this strategy is that you need to reverse what has been done in order to find the answer. For example, if addition is used to go from the original amount to the ending amount, then subtraction is needed to solve the problem. This is a great strategy for helping students understand inverse operations. Although many of these problems can be solved using algebra, Work Backwards is often a more efficient way to get to a solution and is more appropriate for younger learners.

Using the Strategy

To solve Work Backwards problems, you will usually begin with the answer, which is provided, and methodically undo what was done in the problem. Although there are various approaches to working backwards, writing an open sentence with the original conditions of the problem is one way to determine how to work backwards. Drawing a picture or diagram of the actions of the problem and then working back to the original amount is another way to solve the problem.

It is often helpful to write the actions of the problem numerically, leaving the starting number blank and ending with the answers. Look at the following problems:

> Kenny took some money out of his bank. He spent 50¢ at the store and had $1.75 left. How much money did he have to begin with?

$$\$\underline{\hspace{2em}} - \$0.50 = \$1.75$$

In order to determine what he had to start with, you would have to put the 50¢ back, or add it to the $1.75.

$$\$1.75 + \$0.50 = \$2.25$$

It is always a good idea to check the solution by working the problem "forward" to be certain that you have correctly reversed all of the actions.

Does $2.25 - $0.50 = $1.75? It checks, so the solution of $2.25 must be correct.

You can also draw a picture or diagram to show the actions of the problem and then work backwards to find the original amount. Look at this example.

> Last night, Mom baked some blueberry muffins for our class picnic. Much to my surprise, my brother ate $\frac{1}{4}$ of the muffins. My dad ate $\frac{2}{3}$ of what was left. Then my little sister found the plate of muffins and ate $\frac{1}{2}$ of what was left. When I went to get the muffins, there were only two left. How many muffins did Mom bake?

Since you know that the amount left is two muffins, can you determine how many muffins each person ate?

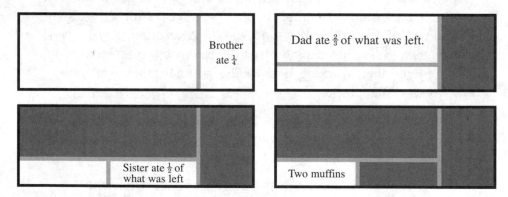

Final Step

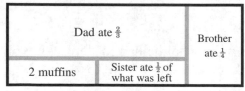

Ready, Set, Solve

Take time to solve the following problems in your journal. Although there are a variety of approaches that can be used, using the Work Backwards strategy will help you to reach a solution efficiently. Notice that in each of these problems, you know the situation at the conclusion of the problem and are asked to identify the start. Think about the actions in the problem and how you would undo each action. Once you reach a solution, redo the problem using your answer and work forward. Do you reach the same final condition as stated in the original problem? Thinking about how you solved the problem and describing your thinking through representations and communication helps to develop a deeper understanding of the process you used to reach a solution. When we focus on the process we used to solve a problem, we can use that process to solve similar problems.

Grades 1–3

Patrick shook the coins out of his piggy bank. He took 25¢ to buy a cool pencil for school. He took 15¢ to buy an eraser. When he counted the money that was left, he still had 45¢. How much money did Patrick have in his piggy bank before he took the coins?

Grades 3–5

Mom just filled the cookie jar with cookies. They were chocolate-chunk cookies—my favorite. My brother came home from soccer practice and took half the cookies. My sister came home from dance lessons and took half of what was left. When my dad got home from work, he took half the remaining cookies. By the time I finished my homework and went downstairs for a snack, there were only two cookies left. How many cookies did mom put in the cookie jar?

Grades 6–8

Dorothy and Toto were on the yellow brick road with a full basket of oranges. When she met the Scarecrow, he was very hungry, so she gave him half of her oranges plus two more. Later she met the Tin Man and gave him half the remaining oranges plus two more. And when she met the Lion she gave him half the remaining oranges plus two more. When they arrived in Oz, Dorothy had two oranges left in her basket. How many oranges were in the basket before Dorothy gave any away?

Change Your Point of View

Understanding the Strategy

Have you ever tried to solve a puzzle or problem, and no matter what you did, you just could not figure it out? Then you put it aside and tackled it a day or two later and you saw the solution immediately? As we approach a problem, we often have one plan and try to make it work. If our plan is not successful, we return to the same point of view and adopt a new plan. Sometimes this works. At other times, we may need to rethink the problem and our approach.

To use the Change Your Point of View strategy, rethink the information in the problem. Discard any previous notions and think outside the box by redefining the problem. This strategy requires a major shift in focus. Elements that initially appeared to be important are down-played, and new ideas get more consideration.

Using the Strategy

This is not an easy strategy to use. Of all the strategies, this one takes the most creative and critical thinking. In fact, many new inventions and ideas are the result of someone entirely changing his or her approach to a problem and starting from scratch with a whole new perspective. The best way to become more comfortable with changing your point of view is to solve a variety of problems that call for divergent thinking. Brain teasers and puzzles are a great way to do this. Although some people may discount the value of these experiences, they inspire creative thinking and higher-order thinking skills.

Here are some ideas for problems that call for Change Your Point of View. You can find them in puzzle books, magazines, and the newspaper, as well as on the Internet. Don't give up if you cannot find a solution. Put the problem away for a while and think about it after a day or two. The more experience you (and your students) have, the better you will get at solving this type of problem.

Toothpick Puzzles

Remove one toothpick to leave 3 squares.

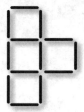

Make this figure with 12 toothpicks.

1. Remove four toothpicks and leave three triangles.

2. Move four toothpicks and form three triangles.

Word Jumbles

Rearrange the letters to make a mathematical word.

nidodait

rgatinel

Sequences

Complete the following sequence:

J, F, M, A, M, J, J, A, S, ___, ___, ___

Brain Teasers

Use four 9s in an equation that equals exactly 100.

Mathematical Puzzles

Arrange 10 trees in five rows, with four trees in each row.

Mathematical Riddles

- Which weighs more: a pound of iron or a pound of feathers?

- Why should you never mention the number 288 in front of anyone?

- A street that is 40 yards long has a tree every 10 yards on both sides. How many total trees are on the entire street?

Ready, Set, Solve

Take time to solve the following problems in your journal. These are tricky, so be prepared to change your point of view! It is very tempting to peek at the solutions, but give yourself some time to think about how you might change your perspective on the problem. Keep track of the development of your thinking in your problem-solving journal. Remember, the more experience you have with these kinds of problems, the better you will become at using this strategy!

Grades K–2

Arrange eight toothpicks in the shape of a fish. Move the toothpicks until the fish is facing another direction. How many toothpicks did you move? Can you do it another way? What is the least number of toothpicks you can move?

Grades 3–5

Complete each of the following sequences.

S, M, T, W, T, _____, _____

O, T, T, F, F ___, ____, _____

F, S, T, F, F, S, S, _____, _____, _____

M, V, E, M, J, S, U, ____, _____

Grade 6–8

A farmer, a fox, a chicken, and a bag of corn must safely cross the river in a very small boat. The farmer may only take one thing at a time in the boat. She cannot leave the fox and the chicken together on either side of the river, because the fox will eat the chicken. And, she cannot leave the chicken alone with the bag of corn, because the chicken will eat the corn. How can the farmer get everything across the river without anything being eaten?

Reflect and Act

Respond to the questions below in your problem-solving journal.

1. Which strategy did you find most useful? Why do you think this is so?

2. Which strategy did you find most difficult? What can you do to become more comfortable with it?

3. Think about using these strategies with your students. How do you think they will react?

CHAPTER 7

Assessing Problem Solving

"Assessment should be more than merely a test at the end of instruction to see how students perform under special conditions; rather, it should be an integral part of instruction that informs and guides teachers as they make instructional decisions. Assessment should not merely be done to students; rather, it should also be done for students, to guide and enhance their learning."

NCTM 2000

As you have read this book, you have begun a learning journey that has helped you and your students to become better problem solvers. On your personal journey, you have stopped to evaluate your thinking—perhaps changed paths in the middle of a problem to reach a solution and continued to think about the mathematical ideas that emerge from the solution process. How do you help your students to develop into good problem solvers? This entails students who can evaluate, revise, and extend their own thinking when faced with a problem-solving situation. Assessing student work is how this begins.

Throw away your preconceived notions of assessment. You need to consider student problem-solving work from many perspectives. Putting a grade on a paper should be the last of your assessment goals. Rather, when you assess a student's attempt at solving a problem, imagine crawling into that student's head to analyze his or her thinking. This includes how the work was organized, the efficient use of strategies, and the mathematical accuracy. Focusing on these aspects will provide a much more valuable picture of where that student is and where he or she needs to go than any letter or number grade you could put on the paper.

As a teacher, student assessment is a critical part of your work. There are many reasons to assess and evaluate student work. According to Van de Walle et al. (2009), "problem solving provides ongoing assessment data that can be used to make instructional decisions, help students succeed, and inform parents." Assessing student thinking through problem solving is much more complex than grading a traditional page of mathematical exercises.

Stop and Think

Respond to the question below in your problem-solving journal.

- Problem solving is the first standard for mathematical practice in the Common Core Standards (2010) and the first process standard in NCTM's *Principles and Standards for School Mathematics* (2000). Why is problem solving so essential to mathematics teaching and learning?

To teach problem solving well takes a great deal of effort on the part of the teacher and much valuable class time. To do problem solving well also takes a great deal of effort from the student. It is difficult to put that kind of effort into something you do not truly believe to be important. Remember, we assess what we value, and we value what is important!

Assessment is an integral part of mathematics instruction. It is through assessment that we improve both student learning and our teaching. Through using a variety of assessments, students have the opportunity to demonstrate what they know and what they still need to learn. *Formative assessments* help teachers to adjust their instruction to meet the needs of students based on immediate feedback. *Summative assessments* tell us what a student has accomplished and mastered over a period of time. Both types of assessment are essential to successful problem solving as well as the development of mathematical thinking through problem-solving experiences (Van De Walle et al. 2009).

Formative Assessment

The term "formative assessment" has several interpretations. To be consistent, consider the definition provided by the Chief Council of State School Officers (2010):

"Formative assessment is a process used by teachers and students during instruction that provides feedback to adjust ongoing teaching and learning to improve students' achievement of intended instructional outcomes."

This definition includes several important ideas. First, this type of assessment is not "done to" students by teachers. True formative assessment is a joint venture in which both the teacher and the student should have an active role. Student participation in assessment happens while the student is solving the problem. There are self-directed questions that should become a habit for students while they are in the process of solving the problem.

- Am I making progress toward a solution, or should I reconsider the strategies I am using?

- Does my work make sense?

- Can I explain and justify it to someone else?

Formative Assessment Using the Launch, Explore, Summarize Instructional Model

Teacher-initiated formative assessment takes place during each phase of instruction in the Launch, Explore, Summarize Instructional Model. In the Launch phase, you determine if students have unpacked the information in the problem and have an entry into finding a solution. You gather information by watching students. Those eager to proceed need little intervention. Some students may have some clarifying questions, after which they can get started. If there are students who are totally lost, you use this information to scaffold the problem to meet their needs. Knowing how to do this is important because you need to discern if it is a comprehension or a mathematics issue. In the former case, you need to back up to the questions students answered to help set the stage for what is happening in the problem. If the issue is with the mathematics, you may need to adjust the problem by using simpler numbers, simplifying the situation, or asking questions to help the student get started. The goal of assessment in the Launch phase of the lesson is to be sure the students are able to get started!

In the Explore phase of the lesson, students are working independently or in groups. As you circulate around the room, be aware of what each group is doing to reach a solution. You are constantly assessing as you observe group or individual work. At first, you may want to ask questions to determine how students are doing. Eventually, you will be able to observe, assess, and for groups that do not need your intervention, move on.

Some ways to assess during the Explore phase include:

- Ask a group member to explain the work and thinking of the group.

- Observe the way students are working with concrete materials and their written representation of the solution process.

  - If they are on the right track, move to another group.

  - If they are stuck, a question to help them proceed (without telling them what to do) is in order.

  - If they are headed in a wrong direction, ask a question that will give them just enough information to think about their work so that they can reconsider what they are doing and think about another possible path.

Remember that your role here should be to observe. The questions you ask students or groups should be for the purpose of assessing their understanding and progress. You will learn a lot from listening and much less from telling!

In the Summarize phase of the lesson, you will be looking for things such as the following:

- efficiency of the strategies students used

- accuracy of the mathematics that students did to solve the problem

- any patterns or generalizations students have discovered

- how students respond to the work of a group who may have approached the problem differently

By assessing these areas, you will be able to determine how to bring the problem and the mathematics to closure for the students by helping them to make their thoughts explicit and to find the connections with other mathematical ideas.

Using Notes and Observations to Assess

Written notes and observations are one way of assessing student work. A page with a list of students' names and space to take notes about each student's work on a problem or task will provide information on whether the student needs additional experience with a concept or a strategy. Using a separate page for each problem allows you to collect a great deal of information on students and to monitor their progress as they gain experience in solving problems and applying strategies.

A Closer Look at Student Thinking

Notice that you move in and out of instruction and assessment. With each question you ask, you assess student understanding to determine where the student is and how much additional support he or she needs to continue. Write notes as you ask the questions and record student responses to aid you through this process. The final goal is to have the student become less dependent on your help to approach a solution process, even when it is not clear, by asking himself or herself the right questions.

Consider the following problem:

> Martina has a new mailbox. She wants to paint her house address on it. The digits she needs to use are 2, 7, and 6. She uses each digit once. What could Martina's address be? How many different addresses are possible using these digits?

Assessing Comprehension Difficulties

Ask the student to read the problem aloud. If there are words that are posing difficulty, help with those words. Some words, such as *digit, different,* and *once* are critical to reaching a solution. Students must be clear on what these words mean in order to have an entry into the problem.

Ask the student to rephrase the problem situation in his or her own words. If the student is not successful, ask him or her to read the problem again and help dissect the problem one sentence at a time.

Assessing Mathematics Difficulties

If students are really struggling with approaching this problem, you might simplify it by starting with two digits. Another scaffolding strategy would be to write the digits 2, 7, and 6 on different slips of paper. Ask the student to show one possible address. Ask how the papers can be rearranged to show another address. Let students continue with the process.

Ask the student how he or she knows that all of the possibilities have been found. This leads to a conversation about organizing the solutions in a logical way.

How to Handle Student Frustration

The kind of problem solving and mathematical understanding that we aspire to with problem-solving instruction can be very frustrating for students—especially in the beginning. Students in the upper grades who have never experienced real problem solving are accustomed to doing the mathematics, getting the answer, and being done. Having to think differently or work in a situation in which the solution process is not immediately obvious often causes students to want to give up. It is important to be explicit as strategies are introduced. Model the problem-solving examples, and inform students of what you value when you are assessing their work. Focusing on progress in thinking and not just with the answer will help students to become proficient in making sense out of a mathematical situation and encourage them to try a variety of approaches when solving a problem. Students will become strategic thinkers, extending their skills beyond the problems they are solving and into all aspects of learning mathematics.

Formative assessment is an important part of the work of teaching. When you ask students a question or observe them working, you are assessing their understanding, which influences your next teaching moves. If the students are on the right track, they can continue with no intervention from you. If students are stuck, you need to determine your next move. What question can you ask to give them just enough information to help move them forward, or should you let them struggle a bit longer to see what progress they can make on their own? Only through formative assessment can you make the decisions you need to inform your instruction. There is no recipe for how to do this. The more you purposefully ask questions, observe students, listen to their thinking, or read their work, the better you will become at learning about their progress and making instructional decisions.

When to Assess

Throughout the lesson

Problem solving can be an individual endeavor, a group activity, or a whole-class lesson. No matter what the organizational scheme of your lesson, assessment is a vital component as you observe, listen, and ask questions.

Written work

After students have had problem-solving experiences in the classroom, assign problems for them to solve outside the mathematics class. This may be homework or a problem of the week with extended time to work. You could provide time to get started in class and have students finish on their own. This type of assessment, though still formative, includes more formal feedback, perhaps in the form of a rubric score.

During class discussions

Listening to students explain their thinking and respond to other students' ideas is a valuable way to determine if they understand a concept. This will help you to decide what to do next, how to divide students to continue the work, or how to differentiate the lesson to meet the needs of individual students.

Student Self-Assessment

Having students assess their own work is the key to formative assessment. Not only does it help students to understand your criteria for their work but it also gives them the opportunity to develop criteria around what they value in their work. Students who take self-assessment seriously can offer you insight into what they understand or what they are struggling with. It is important to take student self-assessment seriously so that your students will take it seriously too. Using students' assessments in a checklist or rubric form during conferences with students and parents provides information about how the students perceive their work. There are several templates of student assessment rubrics included later in this chapter and in Appendix B.

Part of self-assessment includes students' ability to evaluate their work and decide whether they are pleased with the outcome. It is interesting that, in many subject areas, we give students the opportunity to put together their ideas and submit a draft. After we comment on the draft, we offer students the chance to rewrite and resubmit—often until they are satisfied with the final product. Yet we seldom do this in mathematics. Consider allowing your students to make drafts of their problem-solving work so that they can receive feedback from you as well as assess the outcome themselves. They may even do the rewrite following the Summarize phase of the lesson so they can incorporate the new ideas and understandings they have from listening to others.

Summative Assessment

Determining a students' mastery of a particular concept or skill is done through summative assessment. Although formative assessment is used more often in problem-solving situations, after students have had many experiences with solving problems and applying mathematical concepts, you must determine their level of understanding and mastery.

One way to think about formative and summative assessment is with a cooking metaphor. When you try a new recipe, you taste and adjust the food. That is formative assessment. When you serve the meal to your family and get feedback, that is summative assessment.

Stop and Think

Respond to the questions below in your problem-solving journal.

Earlier in this book, you wrote about the characteristics of a good problem solver and why problem solving is important. Go back and take a look at your reflections. Make a list of what you look for when you assess student work. Then, next to each item on your list, note the type of assessment you would use to get that information: formative, summative, or both.

Using Rubrics to Assess

Up to now, we have been talking about formative assessment that is somewhat spontaneous. You listen, ask questions, observe, and gather information from students throughout the lesson and adjust instructional moves based on that information.

How a student represents his or her thinking through written and oral experiences, communicates his or her ideas about a mathematical concept, makes connections among mathematical ideas, and justifies his or her mathematical ideas not only tells you whether the student "can do the mathematics" but also provides information about the student's level and depth of understanding of mathematical concepts. This is when the use of a rubric, which provides more specific criteria for more formal assessment, can be used for either formative or summative assessment purposes.

This book contains some sample rubrics that can be used to help assess students' understanding of a problem-solving strategy and the mathematical concepts being explored through the problem itself, as well as students' ability to organize and clearly communicate their solution. Ideally, you want to reach the point at which you can design your own rubric so that both you and your students know what is valued in problem solving. However, starting with a simple and straightforward rubric will help you to feel more comfortable assessing student problem-solving work.

Begin with the general rubric. As you and your students become comfortable with the general expectations of problem-solving work, it can be modified to fit the characteristics of the problem, including the use of specific strategies, the development of mathematical concepts, and the application of mathematical processes that you may want to see in each student's work. The general rubric (figure 7.1) can be used with students at all grade levels. A simplified version for young students (figure 7.2) is included so that they can become comfortable with the valued components of a good problem solution. Full-size versions of these rubrics can be found in Appendix B.

States that have open response items on their assessments often have samples of released items and the rubrics they used to score student responses. Check your state department of education website and the sites of other states to find examples. You will likely find that the criteria are similar to those we have talked about.

It is important to help students understand the rubric you will use to assess their work so that they understand your expectations. Showing student-work examples of both acceptable and unacceptable solutions also helps students to understand the rubric and your expectations.

Figure 7.1. General Rubric

Criteria	Level One (Novice)	Level Two (Apprentice)	Level Three (Practitioner)	Level Four (Expert)
Organization of Information	• Random • Incomplete • Missing elements	• Mostly complete • Hit-and-miss approach • Most elements are present	• All elements represented • Shows a plan or appropriate strategy • Organized	• Well-planned • Complete and displayed in an organized fashion
Mathematical Accuracy	• Major errors in computation and explanation	• Chose appropriate mathematical concept but unable to accurately complete the task	• Minor errors in computation but demonstrates conceptual understanding	• Accurate
Use of Strategies	• Lack of strategic approach to task • No explanation	• Some demonstration of strategic approach but incomplete or lack of follow through • No representation or explanation	• Shows some application of strategies but not efficient • Some use of representation and or explanation	• Use of efficient and appropriate strategy or combination of strategies • Includes a complete representation or explanation

Summary:

Organization of Information   Level 1 ___   Level 2 ___   Level 3 ___   Level 4 ___

Mathematical Accuracy   Level 1 ___   Level 2 ___   Level 3 ___   Level 4 ___

Use of Strategies   Level 1 ___   Level 2 ___   Level 3 ___   Level 4 ___

Notes:

_____

_____

_____

Figure 7.2. K-2 General Rubric

(applies to written or oral work)

Criteria	Level One (Novice)	Level Two (Apprentice)	Level Three (Practitioner)	Level Four (Expert)
Organization of Information	Messy, not finished, not organized ☹	Almost finished 😐	Somewhat organized and finished ☺	Complete, neat, organized 😁
Mathematical Accuracy	Not correct, not on the right track ☹	On the right track but not correct 😐	Almost correct, some missing pieces ☺	Correct 😁
Use of Strategies	No use of a plan ☹	Use of a plan but did not get to a solution 😐	Some application of a plan shown by work or explanation ☺	Good use of a plan (written or oral) 😁

Summary:

Organization of Information	Level 1 ___	Level 2 ___	Level 3 ___	Level 4 ___
Mathematical Accuracy	Level 1 ___	Level 2 ___	Level 3 ___	Level 4 ___
Use of Strategies	Level 1 ___	Level 2 ___	Level 3 ___	Level 4 ___

Notes:

_____

_____

_____

Final Thoughts

Assessment is an important part of problem solving for several reasons. It helps you to determine the depth of a student's understanding of the mathematics in the problem. Depending on the problem you choose, assessing student work will also give you the information you need to see if the student is making connections to other mathematics and applying the concept to real-life situations. When you use formative assessment strategies in your class, you will have information that will guide your next instructional moves. These strategies also help you to differentiate instruction. You can scaffold your instruction for students who are struggling and extend the mathematics for the students who are ready for more.

Summative assessment provides you the opportunity to assess student learning at specific points in instruction. Although formative assessment is more useful during the problem-solving process, once you expect students to be adept at solving problems around a mathematical concept, summative assessment will help you to evaluate their progress.

This chapter includes models of assessment rubrics and student self-assessment documents. They are designed to get you started. As you feel more comfortable with determining the specifics you are looking for when your students solve a problem, modify the rubric. It is important that students understand your expectations if they are to meet them.

Reflect and Act

Respond to the questions below in your problem-solving journal.

1. How has your understanding of assessing problem solving changed as a result of reading this chapter?

2. Why is student self-assessment an important part of the formative assessment process?

3. Make a list of your goals in assessing student work. Think about the type of assessment that will help you to reach each goal.

CHAPTER 8

Questions from the Field

"It is better to solve one problem five different ways than to solve five different problems."

Polya 2009

In my work with teachers around the country, I have found that many teachers ask similar questions when it comes to effectively implementing problem solving in their classrooms. I have gathered the most frequently asked questions and responded to them here.

Questions About Choosing and Solving Problems

How do I find time to fit problem solving into an already full curriculum?

Look at the mathematics topic that you are teaching. Find a good problem to introduce that topic. This not only gives students an opportunity to explore the topic but also builds and reinforces the application of the mathematics so students can understand why they need to learn it and when they might use it. Use problems to replace some of your "show and tell" lessons with problems that help to build the mathematical understanding.

Where can I find rich problems?

There are many books with rich problems. *Teaching Children Mathematics* and *Mathematics Teaching in the Middle School* are monthly journals published by the National Council of Teachers of Mathematics, and both are loaded with good problems. If you do not belong to the NCTM, your local or district library may subscribe to these journals. You can also find many rich problems on the

Internet, but be careful, as there are also some very poor examples as well. A good place to start is the NCTM *Illuminations* website.

Once you begin to use problems, keep a file of them. Over time, you will build a good library of problems that both you and your students will enjoy solving.

How do I select which problems to use with my students?

You can select problems by the mathematical topic they explore or by the strategy students might use to solve it. If students are just getting started with a strategy-based approach to solving problems, start with problems that will enable them to become comfortable with a specific strategy. Strategy instruction should be explicit. Giving students the opportunity to explore is still important, but discussion on the strategy and good models are critical when strategies are first introduced.

If you are choosing the problem by mathematical content, then you want to look for problems that will develop that concept as students solve it. Developing the habit of analyzing problems for the mathematics they include helps students to hone in on the content.

How do I know what strategy students should use?

Some problems lend themselves to a particular strategy, such as Work Backwards. Most problems can be solved using a variety of strategies or a combination of strategies. When you are getting started, find problems that can be solved with a particular strategy and model with that strategy. When students share their work during the Summarize phase of the lesson, other strategies may come up. Encourage your students to use a variety of strategies. Discuss which strategies are most efficient.

How can I help students to write about their thinking instead of focusing on the answer?

This takes time. For many upper elementary and middle school students, the answer has been the goal in previous mathematics classes. Show that you value the work by setting standards, share models of good work, and emphasize that it is the thinking that goes into solving a problem that is just as important, if not more so, than the answer. It can be helpful to tell students that a week from now, no one will care about the answer, but the process used to solve the problem can be used again in another situation. Be relentless. Make sure that students understand that you value their thinking!

I teach older students. How do I get started with my students who have never used strategies before?

Start at the beginning. Introduce the strategies to your students by giving them problems that employ the strategy. A new strategy each week with a class problem and a homework problem, such as a problem of the week, will get the students familiar with the strategies. The best-case scenario is a problem that also includes the mathematics they are studying. However, that is not always possible. So focus on the strategies first. Once the strategies have been introduced, they are all available for students to use as they solve a variety of problems around the concepts they are learning.

Questions About Confidence and Perseverance

How can I expect my students to solve problems if I do not feel confident about solving problems myself?

Most of us did not learn this kind of problem solving or the use of strategies in our own mathematics education, so we are not as comfortable teaching this way as following the lessons in our mathematics textbooks. The best way to become a good problem solver is to solve problems. This is true for you as well as your students. The problems in this book will get you started. Don't be afraid to learn along with your students. And, don't be surprised if they come up with ways to solve problems that you never thought of. That's wonderful and should be celebrated.

I know problem solving is a critical part of the curriculum and helps students to develop conceptual understanding of important mathematics concepts, but my students are not motivated to think in this way. So, they get to an answer and quit, or they give up when they do not immediately know what to do. What can I do to encourage students to stick with it?

It is really important for *you* to stick with it if you are going to expect your students to stick with it. Find (or edit) problems that are interesting and motivational for your students. Simple ways to get students interested include adding some silliness to the problem or using your students' names in the problem. Also, be sure to include the Summarize phase in your lesson. Without it, students are left hanging and often miss the importance of the strategy or the mathematics. Problems should be challenging enough but not too challenging for students. Most importantly, make sure your expectations for student work are clear and understood. Share good examples of student work. Keep your expectations high, but also reasonable. You want your students to be challenged but not totally frustrated. Finally, remember that a good problem often cannot be solved in one class period. Give students the time they need to be successful.

Questions About Differentiation and Problem Solving

How can I differentiate my instruction with problem solving?

Problem solving is one of the best ways to differentiate mathematics instruction. You can simplify the problem for students who are struggling. This can be done by breaking the problem into steps and asking a question for each step. You can simplify the conditions of the problem. For example, instead of asking how many pieces of candy you need to fill 15 cups if 24 go in each cup, make the numbers simpler. For students who can solve the problem with little effort, be ready with a similar problem that involves taking the mathematics to a higher level. This takes some practice on your part, but you will soon become comfortable at layering a problem to meet the needs of the students in your class.

What can I do to support students who have difficulty comprehending the problem?

Students often think they should be able to solve the problem after reading it once. Use the same comprehension strategies you would use in teaching reading. If it is a vocabulary issue, find the words that may present difficulties and help students to focus on those. If it is a contextual issue, be sure that your students are familiar with the context as part of the Launch phase of the lesson. Asking students to read the problem more than once and put it in their own words works for many students. Be sure that students with comprehension issues are completing the steps in the Polya model. That will also help them to comprehend the problem. For students with serious reading issues, simplify the words of the problem. For young children, use a rebus (pictures) in place of difficult vocabulary that they may not yet know.

What do I do with students who successfully solve a problem before others in the class?

Remember it is just as important for these students to value the thinking process as well as the solution as it is for the other kids in the class. A correct answer with no thinking is not acceptable. (These are often the hardest students to convince!) Their work should be complete, organized, and clear in order to be considered complete. Once that expectation has been met, ask students if there is another way to solve the problem, if there are other possible solutions, and if they have accounted for all possible solutions. Such questions give these students an opportunity to delve deeper into the problem. Extending the problem by adding a layer of complexity to the situation, using more difficult numbers, or adding another step are also ways to help these students extend their thinking about the problem and the mathematical ideas.

How can I incorporate technology in my problem-solving classroom?

Consider the type of technology you might want to use. Allowing students to use calculators may be appropriate for some problems—especially when the mathematics gets "messy." At other times, particularly when you are trying to develop conceptual understanding through modeling or drawing pictures, a calculator is not appropriate. A document camera or interactive whiteboard are excellent ways to have students share their work. If you do not have access to these resources, chart paper can be posted in the classroom.

Questions About Assessment

Can I use problem solving for summative assessment?

Although rich problems are commonly assessed to inform instruction and determine student understanding over time, many states use open response items on their tests. Once students have had experience with problems around a particular mathematics concept, a level of mastery of the concept and its use in an application or context should be expected. That is the time to use a rich problem for summative assessment. As with any other kind of summative assessment, you should have clear expectations, identify the mathematics, and know how you will evaluate (grade) student work.

How do I grade student work?

Grades are an important part of our educational process. They are also a motivating factor for some students. The use of a rubric is the best way to assess student work in problem solving. The rubric should include your goals for using a particular problem and should be clear to the students. You can give a grade based on how students perform under each of the criteria in your rubric. The rubric can be as specific or as general as you want it to be. You might want to start out with a general rubric so that students can focus on the important aspects of problem solving to get started (selecting strategies, organizing their work, mathematical accuracy) and then get more specific depending on your purpose for using a particular problem. A good rule of thumb might be as follows: novice is a *D*, apprentice is a *C*, practitioner is a *B*, and expert is an *A*. However, allow students to submit drafts, rewrite, and rethink. Putting a D on the paper of a student who needs more support and the opportunity to internalize the mathematics can be very defeating and may encourage students to give up. So grade with caution!

Student Journal Templates

Template 1

Problem

What do I want to find out?

_____

_____

What important information do I know?

_____

_____

What else do I need to know?

_____

_____

What extra information is in the problem?

_____

_____

Here is my estimate or prediction:

_____

_____

Strategies I plan to use:

_____

_____

Student Journal Templates

Template 2

My Work

Answer to the question:

_____

_____

Partners who worked with me:

_____

_____

New ideas I learned from solving this problem:

_____

_____

Questions I have about this problem:

_____

_____

Assessment Resources

Student Self-Assessment Rubric

Grades K-2

Criteria	Not Sure	A Good Beginning	Good Job	Super Job
I understand the problem.	☹	😐	🙂	😁
I understand what to do with the math.	☹	😐	🙂	😁
I showed my work neatly and completely.	☹	😐	🙂	😁

Note: Some explanation and examples of the criteria should be provided to students before they complete their self-assessment. Use of the self-assessment tool can take place before and after the Summarize part of the lesson when students have some other work to compare with their own work.

Assessment Resources

Student Self-Assessment Rubric

Grades 2-5

Criteria	Level One (Novice)	Level Two (Apprentice)	Level Three (Practitioner)	Level Four (Expert)
Understands the Problem and the Math	I did not understand the problem.	I understood parts of the problem. I started but did not finish solving the problem.	I understood the problem and reached a reasonable answer. I used some mathematics to solve the problem.	I understood the problem and the mathematics. I can explain my work and the mathematics I used to solve the problem.
Use of Strategies	I could not find a strategy to help me solve the problem.	I tried a strategy but got stuck and did not know how to finish the problem. I needed more help.	I used one or more strategies that helped me to solve the problem.	I used one or more strategies to solve the problem. I used mathematical ideas and extended my thinking to another way to solve, another solution, or another problem.
Organization	I did not show any work and cannot explain how to solve the problem.	I showed my work for as much as I completed. I tried to explain my thinking. My work was not neat and organized.	I clearly explained how I solved the problem. I used some pictures, numbers, or words in my explanation.	I clearly explained how I solved the problem and showed my work with details so that someone can understand exactly what I was thinking. I have included pictures, numbers, or words.

What I learned from solving this problem:

_____

Questions I have:

_____

_____

Assessment Resources

Student Self-Assessment Rubric

Grades 6–8

Criteria	Level One (Novice)	Level Two (Apprentice)	Level Three (Practitioner)	Level Four (Expert)
Organization of Information	My work is incomplete. It is not organized, so it is hard to follow.	My work is somewhat complete. I could have done more to show my thinking.	I have shown all of my work. The strategy I used is clearly shown. My work is organized.	My work is well-planned. It is easy to understand my thinking and what I did to solve the problem. It is complete and organized.
Mathematical Accuracy	I did not understand the mathematics involved in the problem.	I think I knew what to do, but I got stuck somewhere in the process of solving. I could not reach a solution.	I understood the mathematics, but I made some silly mistakes in my computation or math thinking.	I understood the mathematics, showed my steps, and arrived at an accurate solution.
Use of Strategies	I did not know what strategy to use. I did not show any work or explain my thinking.	I started with a strategy but got stuck and did not know where to go next. I could not think of another approach, so I did not reach a solution.	I selected a strategy, but it was not very efficient. It took me a long time to get to a solution. I included some explanation about my approach.	I chose good strategies that led me to a solution. I included all of my work and a clear explanation of what I did.

What I learned from solving this problem:

_____

_____

Questions I still have:

_____

_____

Assessment Resources

General Rubric

Criteria	Level One (Novice)	Level Two (Apprentice)	Level Three (Practitioner)	Level Four (Expert)
Organization of Information	• Random • Incomplete • Missing elements	• Mostly complete • Hit-and-miss approach • Most elements are present	• All elements represented • Shows a plan or appropriate strategy • Organized	• Well-planned • Complete and displayed in an organized fashion
Mathematical Accuracy	• Major errors in computation and explanation	• Chose appropriate mathematical concept but unable to accurately complete the task	• Minor errors in computation but demonstrates conceptual understanding	• Accurate
Use of Strategies	• Lack of strategic approach to task • No explanation	• Some demonstration of strategic approach but incomplete or lack of follow through • No representation or explanation	• Shows some application of strategies but not efficient • Some use of representation and or explanation	• Use of efficient and appropriate strategy or combination of strategies • Includes a complete representation or explanation

Summary:

Organization of Information   Level 1 ___   Level 2 ___   Level 3 ___   Level 4 ___

Mathematical Accuracy   Level 1 ___   Level 2 ___   Level 3 ___   Level 4 ___

Use of Strategies   Level 1 ___   Level 2 ___   Level 3 ___   Level 4 ___

Notes:

_____

_____

_____

Assessment Resources

General Rubric (Grades K-2)
(applies to written or oral work)

Criteria	Level One (Novice)	Level Two (Apprentice)	Level Three (Practitioner)	Level Four (Expert)
Organization of Information	Messy, not finished, not organized	Almost finished	Somewhat organized and finished	Complete, neat, organized
Mathematical Accuracy	Not correct, not on the right track	On the right track but not correct	Almost correct, some missing pieces	Correct
Use of Strategies	No use of a plan	Use of a plan but did not get to a solution	Some application of a plan shown by work or explanation	Good use of a plan (written or oral)

Summary:

Organization of Information Level 1 ___ Level 2 ___ Level 3 ___ Level 4 ___

Mathematical Accuracy Level 1 ___ Level 2 ___ Level 3 ___ Level 4 ___

Use of Strategies Level 1 ___ Level 2 ___ Level 3 ___ Level 4 ___

Notes:

_____

_____

_____

Assessment Resources

Observation Recording Sheet

Problem:

_____

Strategy/Strategies:

_____

Mathematical Ideas:

_____

Student Name	Notes	Follow-Up Actions

Additional Problems for Practice

These problems will give you extra problem-solving opportunities. You should practice solving them in your journal and then choose appropriate problems to use with your students. The problems are categorized by the chapter in which a possible solution strategy was presented, and solutions can be found in Appendix D. Keep in mind that most problems can be solved by a variety of strategies or by using several strategies, so do not limit yourself to just the strategies listed. The goal for you and your students is to become fluent with the strategies and choose ones that are efficient.

Chapter 3: Getting Started Strategies

These are the strategies presented in Chapter 3. Consider using them to solve the problems provided here.

- Restate the Problem

- Identify Wanted, Given, and Needed Information

- Identify a Subgoal

- Select Appropriate Notation

1. Jack and Jill went up the hill to fetch a pail of water. They had a 3-quart bucket and a 5-quart bucket. When they got down to the bottom of the hill, they found an 8-quart bucket. How could they divide the water so that each one had 4 quarts of water?

2. Four students decide to throw a Super Bowl party. They agree to share the expenses equally. Mina buys a cake for $8. Ricardo buys ice cream for $5. Martina spends $2 on popcorn, and Dave gets $3 worth of soft drinks. In addition, Dave pays the $6 needed to rent the giant popcorn popper. To be fair, who owes money to whom?

3. Remember the princess and the pea? She had problems sleeping because of a pea under her mattress. Well, her problem was tiny compared to that of her cousin, the duchess. The duchess bought a radio, got back to the castle, and discovered that it played only rock music. "Horrors!" she gasped. "Where is Beethoven? Where is Mozart? What is all this screaming?" She took the radio back and exchanged it, only to have the same thing happen again. The duchess exchanged quite a few radios before she found one that would pick up a classical station back at the castle. She was glad the radio was on her Chopin Liszt, and she would be certain to Handel it with care, so she wouldn't have to take this one Bach. You might be wondering how many radios the duchess took back before she found the right one. Here is a clue: The total number of radios divided in half, added to 9, equals three-fourths the number of radios. How many radios did the duchess return?

4. Jacob, Jonathan, Josh, Jason, and George were the first five to cross the finish line of the 10K race. Use these clues to find the order in which they finished.

   - Jacob passed Jonathan just before the finish line.

   - George finished 10 seconds ahead of Jacob.

   - Josh crossed the finish line in a dead heat with Jonathan.

   - Jason was fifth at the finish.

5. Nihal drew the following diagram to show his friends' favorite sports.

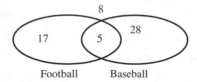

Football   Baseball

How many people were asked? How many like baseball? Football? Both? Neither? Explain your thinking.

6. Ruth has 12 markers in her desk. One third of them are blue and one fourth of them are red. The rest are green. How many of each color does she have?

7. The Empire State Building in New York City is 1,453 feet, 9 inches tall. How many 3-inch long toothpicks would it take to reach from the ground to the top of the Empire State Building?

8. The village of Roses is known for its beautiful gardens. The gardens are built in a very interesting pattern shown below. The Norris family wants to build a very large garden in their backyard. They have enough room for an eight-plot garden. What are the area and the perimeter of their garden?

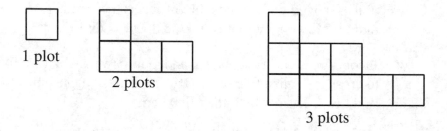

1 plot

2 plots

3 plots

9. Laron and Jeff are earning money by shoveling snow. Laron charges $7.50 an hour. Jeff charges $5 an hour for the first 3 hours and then $9 an hour for each hour after that. How many hours does Jeff have to work to earn more money than Laron?

10. My house number is a three-digit number. Each digit is different. It is an even number. It is divisible by 3. It is the closest number to 600 that fits these clues. What is my house number?

Chapter 4: Getting Organized Strategies

These are the strategies presented in Chapter 4. Consider using them to solve the problems provided here.

- Look for a Pattern

- Create a Table

- Create an Organized List

- Guess and Check

1. Lashay has some pennies. When she counts them by fives, there are three left over. When she counts them by sevens, there are two left over. She has almost $1.00 in pennies. How many pennies does Lashay have?

2. Who am I?

   - The sum of my digits is greater than 8.

   - The difference between my digits is 1.

   - I can be evenly divided by 8.

   - I am an even number less than 100.

3. Bozo has $1.07 in coins. He cannot make change for $1.00. He cannot make change for 25¢. He cannot make change for 10¢. He has exactly 7 coins. What coins does he have?

4. If you start at the number 1 and count by 3s, you get the following sequence:

   $$1, 4, 7, 10, 13 \ldots$$

   What is the 100th number in this sequence?

5. The Lazy Lizards, a rock band, will appear in concert tonight. Fans began arriving in groups. The first group had only Patsy in it. She arrived very early. Each group after that had two more people than the group that arrived before it. How many people attended the concert if 20 groups came in all?

6. Find a set of three consecutive even numbers whose sum is 216.

Find a set of four consecutive odd numbers whose sum is 216.

Find a set of three consecutive numbers whose sum is 216.

What do you notice?

7. There are 20 students collecting the golf balls that have fallen into the water trap and then selling them for practice balls. The first student brought in one golf ball. The second student sold the ball. The third student brought in three golf balls, and the fourth student sold one. The fifth student brought in five golf balls, and the sixth student sold one. This continues as every odd number student brings in the same number of golf balls as his or her number, while the even numbered students sell one golf ball each. When all 20 students have finished, how many golf balls will be unsold?

8. Prince Charming is slaying dragons. He must slay 50 dragons in one day to rescue the maiden in distress. If he slays four dragons the first day, nine dragons the second day, 14 dragons the third day, and continues with this pattern, how long will it be before he rescues the fair maiden?

9. During a football game, your team scored 15 points. In how many different ways could your team have made that score? Remember:

- A touchdown scores 6 points

- An extra point after a touchdown scores 1 point

- A field goal scores 3 points

- A safety scores 2 points

10. The Wolfe family has their activities planned for the summer. On the first day, they will go swimming. On the second day, they will go to the park. On the third day, they will play baseball. On the fourth day, they will go to the library. On the fifth day, they will go swimming. On the sixth day, they will go to the park. On the seventh day, they will play baseball, and on the eighth day, they will go to the library. If they continue this pattern, what will they do on the 21st day of summer? What will they do on the 31st day?

11. Arrange the numbers from 1 to 6 in the circles below so that the sum of the numbers along each side of the triangle is 10. How many different solutions can you find?

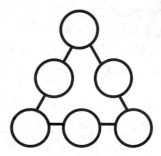

Chapter 5: Visualizing Strategies

These are the strategies presented in Chapter 5. Consider using these to solve the problems provided here.

- Make a Model
- Draw a Picture or Diagram
- Act It Out
- Make or Use a Graph

1. Huge Harold took $\frac{2}{3}$ of a pizza but could only eat half of the portion. Little Lucy took $\frac{1}{2}$ of a pizza but could only eat two-thirds of her portion. Who ate more?

2. Mrs. Math baked chocolate chip cookies for the class party. She put eight cookies in each of 24 bags, one bag for each student. There were four cookies left over. How many cookies did Mrs. Math bake?

3. You need 27 cubes (nine each of three colors). How can you arrange them into a larger cube so that no row has a repeated color and no column has a repeated color?

4. A frog fell to the bottom of a 20-foot well. Each day he climbed up five feet. However, each evening he was very tired and slid back two feet. If the frog continued with this pattern, how long would it take him to get out of the well?

5. Michele and Devonte like to trade. They agree that six peanuts are worth two apples and 10 apples are worth five bananas. How many peanuts should Devonte give Michele in trade for three bananas?

6. If you fold a sheet of paper in half 10 times, how many layers of paper will be on top of each other?

7. An explorer spotted 30 animals in the jungle: 17 had fur, 21 had tails, and two had neither fur nor a tail. Of all the animals the explorer saw, how many had both fur and a tail?

8. Anna and Monika like to swim laps at the community pool. They are swimming together today, but they are on different schedules. Anna swims every three days, and Monika swims every five days. How many times will their schedules coincide over the next 10 weeks?

9. At a party, Mrs. Square asked Mrs. Circle, "How many children do you have, and what are their ages?" Mrs. Circle replied, "I have three children. The product of their ages is 36, and the sum of their ages is equal to the address of this house." Mrs. Square walked outside and looked at the house address. She found Mrs. Circle and said, "I need just a bit more information." Mrs. Circle replied, "I'm sorry, but I have to leave. My oldest child is babysitting and needs me to come home." After Mrs. Circle left, Mrs. Square thought, "I know the ages of her children!" What are the ages of Mrs. Circle's children?

10. When Snow White married Prince Charming and moved into his castle, the seven dwarfs sold their cottage and scattered to different parts of the country. Four moved to the West Coast and opened a diamond store. Three moved to the East Coast and bought a clothing store that sold half-sizes. Four of the dwarfs bought condominiums by the beach, and three bought houses in the city. Grouchy, Joyful, and Wheezy moved to the same coast. Silly and Nosy moved to different coasts. Silly, Snoozy, and Shy bought the same kind of home, but Joyful and Nosy purchased different kinds of homes. One day, a royal messenger brought Snow White the news that one of the dwarfs who lived in a house on the East Coast was getting married. Snow White sent the dwarf a letter offering the castle for the wedding. To which dwarf did she address the letter?

Chapter 6: Reasoning Strategies

These are the strategies presented in Chapter 6. Consider using these to solve the problems provided here.

- Solve a Simpler Problem

- Account for All Possibilities

- Work Backwards

- Change your Point of View

1. How many different rectangles are in this figure?

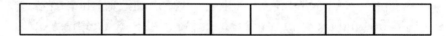

2. Liness has to be at school at 8:30 A.M. It takes her 30 minutes to shower and get dressed, 20 minutes to eat breakfast, and five minutes to walk to the bus stop. The bus ride to school is 15 minutes long. What time does Liness need to wake up?

3. Jane has pennies, nickels, and dimes in her purse:

- She has 8 coins altogether.

- She has fewer nickels than dimes.

- She has fewer pennies than nickels.

How much money could she have?

4. Mom bought a giant chocolate bar and cut it into equal pieces. If Gina eats $\frac{1}{3}$ of the pieces and Carla eats $\frac{1}{2}$ of the remaining pieces, there are 12 pieces left over. Into how many pieces did Mom originally cut the chocolate bar?

5. Caleb loves to go shopping. As soon as he gets his allowance, he heads for the mall. Yesterday, he used his allowance to buy some jeans. In the first store, he spent half his money and three dollars more. Then, he went to buy a shirt, and in that store, he spent half his remaining money and two dollars more. After he bought the jeans and the shirt, he had five dollars left. How much allowance did Caleb receive?

6. A regular bowling alley has the pins set like this:

There are four rows with one pin in the first row and four pins in the last row. You hit a "strike" when you knock down all 10 pins with one ball.

The new MegaBowl has decided the game would be much more interesting if they added six more rows following the same pattern. How many pins would you have to knock down with one ball in order to get a strike at the MegaBowl?

7. Alex, who always has a scheme for everything, has just made a deal with his parents. He told them that rather than paying $10 a week for his allowance, they can pay him in a different way. He asks for one cent on the first day, two cents on the second day, four cents on the third day, and so on, with each day's pay being double the pay of the previous day. If Alex's parents fall for his scheme, how much allowance will Alex receive after two weeks?

8. Marvin baked some brownies. He gave half of them to some of the first-graders out at recess. He gave $\frac{1}{4}$ of what was left to the third-graders in the hallway. After he gave 6 away at lunchtime, he had no brownies left. How many brownies did Marvin bake?

9. One night the king couldn't sleep, so he went down into the royal kitchen where he found a basket full of grapes. He was hungry, so he ate $\frac{1}{6}$ of the grapes. Later that night, the queen was hungry, and she couldn't sleep. She went down to the royal kitchen, found the basket of grapes, and ate $\frac{1}{5}$ of what was left. Still later, the prince awoke, went down to the kitchen, and ate $\frac{1}{4}$ of the grapes that were left. Even later, his sister, the princess, woke up and went down to the kitchen. She found the basket of grapes and ate $\frac{1}{3}$ of the grapes in the basket. Finally, the royal dog came by and saw the grapes. He ate $\frac{1}{2}$ of the remaining grapes. The next morning, the cook came down to make breakfast for the royal family. There were only three grapes left in the basket. How many grapes were originally in the basket?

10. If it costs 5¢ each time you cut and weld a link, what is the least amount you can pay to make a chain out of the five links?

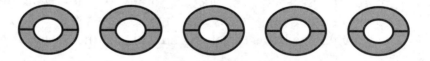

Answer Key

Chapter 3 Solutions

Restate the Problem in Your Own Words

Ready, Set, Solve (p. 76)

A pen, a pencil, and an eraser cost $2.70 altogether. The pencil was $1.00 more than the eraser. The pen was $0.30 more than the pencil and eraser together. How much was the pen?

The pen, the pencil, and the eraser cost $2.70, so that is the total bill. The pencil costs $1.00 more than the eraser. If the eraser cost 5¢, the pencil would be $1.05. The pen was 30¢ more than the pencil and the eraser, so if the eraser was 5¢ and the pencil was $1.05, the pen would be $1.45. To find the cost of the pen, use this information:

Eraser Cost	Pencil Cost (eraser + $1.00)	Pen Cost (pencil + eraser + 30¢)	Total Cost
5¢	$1.05	$1.40	$2.50
10¢	$1.10	$1.50	$2.70

The cost of the pen was $1.50.

While counting her money, Beth noticed that she had the same number of dimes as nickels, and the same number of quarters as nickels. How many nickels did she have if her coins were worth $2.00?

The number of dimes is the same as the number of nickels. The number of quarters is the same as the number of nickels. That means the number of nickels, dimes, and quarters is all the same. The coins are worth $2.00. How many nickels does she have?

Nickels	Dimes	Quarters	Total
1	1	1	5¢ + 10¢ + 25¢ = 40¢ (too low)
3	3	3	15¢ + 30¢ + 75¢ = $1.20 (too low)
5	5	5	25¢ + 50¢ + $1.25 = $2.00 (got it!)

She had five nickels.

One year, one-fifth of the children in Miss Baker's class had perfect attendance records. Of the children, 28 did not have perfect attendance records. How many children were in the class?

If $\frac{1}{5}$ of the students had perfect attendance, that means $\frac{4}{5}$ did not have perfect attendance. There were 28 students that did not have perfect attendance. So, $\frac{4}{5}$ = 28. How many students were in the class?

If $\frac{4}{5}$ = 28, than $\frac{1}{5}$ would have to be 7, since 4 × 7 = 28. 28 + 7 = 35.

28 students

There were 35 students in Miss Baker's class.

Identify Wanted, Given, and Needed Information

Understanding the Strategy (p. 77)

Every item at Hardware Heaven was marked down an additional 25%. The electric drill was originally $68.00 and was marked down 15%. How much did the drill cost?

The problem needs information that requires me to do something with the facts given before I can finally get its solution.

George Washington died on December 14, 1799. How old was he when he died?

The problem needs information that I may be able to find through another source before I solve it.

How many children under the age of 12 visited the observation deck of the Empire State Building last month?

The problem needs information which is not known or available to me. Therefore, I cannot solve it.

Ready, Set, Solve (p. 79)

One pipe can fill a tank in three hours, and another pipe can fill the tank in six hours. How long will it take to fill the tank if both pipes are used at the same time?

Wanted: How long will it take to fill the tank?

Given: One pipe fills the tank in three hours and another fills it in six hours.

Needed: How long will it take the pipes together to fill the tank?

I can find out by making a model and trying some different numbers.

Time	Pipe A	Pipe B	Amount Filled
1 hour	$\frac{1}{3}$ tank	$\frac{1}{6}$ tank	$\frac{3}{6}$ or $\frac{1}{2}$ tank
2 hours	$\frac{2}{3}$ tank	$\frac{2}{6}$ tank	$\frac{6}{6}$ or full tank

It would take 2 hours to fill the tank.

Susan, her brother, her daughter, and her son all went bike riding. The fastest and slowest riders were the same age, while the slowest rider's twin was slower than the fastest. If Susan rode faster than her children, who rode the fastest?

Wanted: Who rode the fastest: Susan, her brother, her daughter, or her son?

Given: The fastest and slowest were the same age. The slowest rider's twin was slower than the fastest. Susan rode faster than her children.

Needed: I need to figure out the relationships based on the information in the problem.

Susan rode faster than her children so that she would have to be first or second.

Susan cannot be the same age as her children.

Susan's daughter and son must have been twins, based on the clue that the slowest rider's twin was slower than the fastest.

So, Susan's brother must have been the same age as the twins and was the fastest.

(#4) Slowest	(#3)	(#2)	(#1) Fastest
Son	Daughter	Susan	Brother

There are seven girls (including Ling) living on Ling's street. The average of their ages is 13. One of the girls is 16 years old, and four of the girls are two years under the average. What is Ling's age if the other girl is 13?

Wanted: Ling's age.

Given: There are seven girls on the street. The average of their ages is 13. One girl is 16, and there are four girls who are 11 (two years under the average). The other girl is 13.

186

Needed: What do I need to add to the information I have to make the average 13?

The average is the sum of their ages divided by 7. I need to find out what the sum of their ages should be.

$$7 \times 13 = 91 \quad \text{(the total of their ages)}$$

$$16 + 11 + 11 + 11 + 11 + 13 + \text{Ling} = 91$$

$$16 + 11 + 11 + 11 + 11 + 13 = 73 + \text{Ling} = 91$$

$$91 - 73 = 18$$

Ling is 18 years old.

I can check by adding:

$$16 + 11 + 11 + 11 + 11 + 13 + 18 = 91$$

$$91 \div 7 = 13$$

Identify a Subgoal

Ready, Set, Solve (p. 81)

Mr. and Mrs. Jogger like to run. From past experiences they know that Mr. Jogger can run 6 km in the time it takes Mrs. Jogger to cover 4 km. They would like to run the same distance, 9 km, and finish together. How much of a head start does Mrs. Jogger need for them to finish together?

Start by figuring out how far each runs in 30 minutes.

Time	Mrs. Jogger runs	Mr. Jogger runs
$\frac{1}{2}$ hour	2	3
1 hour	4	6
$1\frac{1}{2}$ hours	6	9

In $1\frac{1}{2}$ hours Mrs. Jogger will cover 6 km. She needs a 3 km head start to finish with Mr. Jogger.

During one school year, Stella was given 25¢ for each math test she passed and was fined 50¢ for each math test she failed. By the end of the school year, Stella passed seven times as many math tests as she failed and she had a total of $3.75. How many tests did she fail?

Stella gets 25¢ for each test she passes and has to pay 50¢ for each test she fails.

She passed seven times as many tests as she failed and had a total of $3.75. I want to know how many tests she failed.

Start with seven tests passed and one test failed to see how much she makes.

Tests Passed	Money Earned	Tests Failed	Money Paid	Total Money Earned
7	7 × 25¢ = $1.75	1	50¢	$1.25

For each group of seven tests passed and one test failed, Stella earns $1.25. Since she earned a total of $3.75, that means she took three groups of tests, or she passed 21 tests and failed three tests. (You can also solve this by continuing the table.)

Check: 21 tests passed ($5.25) and three tests failed (–$1.50) leaves Stella with $3.75.

Stella failed 3 tests.

Use the diagram to fill in the numbers using these clues:

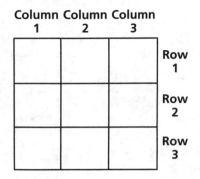

- *Each digit 1–9 is used once.*
- *Row 1 is half the total of Column 1.*
- *Row 1 contains the prime factorization of 30.*
- *There are no composite numbers in Column 3.*
- *The sums of Column 3 and Row 2 are the same.*
- *Column 2 contains even and consecutive numbers.*
- *All corner numbers are odd and consecutive.*
- *There is a square number in each column.*

Look at each clue and build a list of information you can use to solve the problem. Each clue is a subgoal.

Clue	What I Know
1. Each digit 1–9 is used once.	1 2 3 4 5 6 7 8 9
2. Row 1 is half the total of Column 1.	The sum of row 1 is 10 (Clue 3)
3. Row 1 contains the prime factorization of 30.	$2 \times 3 \times 5$ are in Row 1; 3 and 5 are in the corners (Clue 7)
4. There are no composite numbers in Column 3.	1, 2, 3, 5, or 7 are in Column 3
5. The sums of Column 3 and Row 2 are the same.	The clue can be used to check your answer.
6. Column 2 is even and consecutive.	Could be 2, 4, 6, or 4, 6, 8
7. All corner numbers are odd and consecutive.	Are 1, 3, 5, 7, or 3, 5, 7, 9
8. There is a square number in each column.	1, 4, or 9 are in each Column 4 must be in Column 2

Column 1 Column 2 Column 3

3	2	5	Row 1
8	4	1	Row 2
9	6	7	Row 3

190

Select Appropriate Notation

Ready, Set, Solve (p. 84)

The students at Linda's party are playing a new game. They are seated around a circular table, evenly spaced and consecutively numbered. Linda is number 5. She is directly opposite Kim who is number 16. How many students are at the party?

To solve this problem, draw a picture and fill in what you know.

Start by putting Linda in seat 5 and Kim across from her in seat 16. If they are directly across from each other, there are 10 seats between them on either side. Draw in the other seats (or add 10 + 10 + 2) and you will find there are 22 people playing the game.

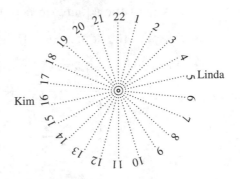

Another notation would be to make a list. If seat 5 is across from 16, then you can work up and down from the information you know to find that: Since 1 is across from 12, and 11 is across from 22, there are 22 players.

There are also some interesting patterns that come from this problem!

In this tangram puzzle, you can make many different shapes by putting the seven pieces together in different ways.

If the area of the entire puzzle is one square unit, find the area of each of the pieces.

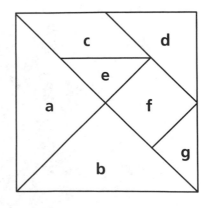

If you divide the puzzle so that all of the pieces are the same size (equivalent to the size of pieces *e* and *g*), you will find you have 16 pieces:

- *a* is $\frac{4}{16}$ of the square or $\frac{1}{4}$ unit^2
- *b* is $\frac{4}{16}$ of the square or $\frac{1}{4}$ unit^2
- *c* is $\frac{2}{16}$ of the square or $\frac{1}{8}$ unit^2
- *d* is $\frac{2}{16}$ of the square or $\frac{1}{8}$ unit^2
- *e* is $\frac{1}{16}$ of the square or $\frac{1}{16}$ unit^2
- *f* is $\frac{2}{16}$ of the square or $\frac{1}{8}$ unit^2
- *g* is $\frac{1}{16}$ of the square or $\frac{1}{16}$ unit^2

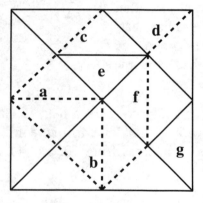

To check, you can add all of the fractions. The sum is $\frac{16}{16}$, or 1 unit.

The Wright Brothers have a collection of bicycle seats and wheels. They have a total of 26 seats and 60 wheels. They decide to make some bicycles, tricycles, and unicycles. There are more bicycles than any other type of cycles. The number of wheels they put on bicycles is close to the number of wheels they put on the tricycles. They do not use very many wheels to make the unicycles. How many of each type of cycle do they make?

I know that they have 26 seats and 60 wheels.   **seats   wheels**

Unicycles have one seat and one wheel   ○   ○

Bicycles have one seat and two wheels   ○   ○○

Tricycles have one seat and three wheels   ○   ○○○

Since they all have one seat, I know they made 26 cycles altogether.

The number of bikes is greatest, and they used almost the same number of wheels for tricycles.

They made the least number of unicycles.

Bikes (Wheels)	Tricycles (Wheels)	Unicycles (Wheels)	Total Seats	Total Wheels
10 (20)	7 (21)	9 (9)	26	50
12 (24)	7 (21)	7 (7)	26	52
15 (30)	9 (27)	2 (2)	26	59
14 (28)	10 (30)	2 (2)	26	60

This is one solution. Are there others possible?

Chapter 4 Solutions

Look for a Pattern

Ready, Set, Solve (p. 90)

Grades K-2

Marta is reading a book for her summer reading club. On the first day, she read two pages. On the second day, she read five pages. On the third day, she read eight pages. How many pages did Marta read on the sixth day?

day	1	2	3	4	5	6
pages	2	5	8	11	14	17

Marta read 17 pages on the sixth day. The pattern is adding 3 more pages each day.

Grades 3-5

Our class has a plan for recess time. We would like one minute on the first day of school, two minutes on the second day, four minutes on the third day, eight minutes on the fourth day and so on. If our teacher accepts the plan, how long will recess be at the end of the second week of school? Express your answer in more than one way.

day	1	2	3	4	5	6	7	8	9	10
minutes	1	2	4	8	16	32	64	128	256	512
total time	1	3	7	15	31	63	127	255	511	1,023

There would be 1,023 minutes, or 17 hours and 3 minutes of recess on the tenth day of school!

The pattern is that the number of minutes doubles each day, and the total time for each day is one less than the number of minutes by the next day.

Grades 6-8

Larry is having a party. The first time the doorbell rings, one person enters. Each time the doorbell rings, a group enters that has two more people than the previous group. What is the total number of guests at the party after the doorbell rings 10 times?

Doorbell Ring	People Entering	Total Number
1	1	1
2	3	4
3	5	9
4	7	16
5	9	25
6	11	36
7	13	49
8	15	64
9	17	81
10	19	100

There will be 100 guests at the party after the 10th ring.

The pattern is the number of people who enter is two times the number of rings minus 1 (2 × number of rings – 1). The total is the number of rings squared.

Create a Table

Ready, Set, Solve (p. 94)

Grades K-2

Jonathan wants to buy a candy bar that costs a quarter. He has pennies, nickels, and dimes but no quarters in his pocket. How can he pay for the candy bar with exactly 25¢?

Pennies	Nickels	Dimes
25	0	0
20	1	0
15	2	0
15	0	1
10	3	0
10	1	1
5	4	0
5	2	1
5	0	2
0	5	0
0	3	1
0	1	2

There are 12 different ways that he can make 25¢.

Grades 3-5

Suzanne and Jose work at the city garden in the summer. Suzanne comes every third day to water all of the plants. Jose comes every fifth day to pull weeds. They never miss a day—even on weekends! If they are both working at the garden today, how many times will they be working on the same day in the next six weeks?

	days												
Jose	①	6	11	⑯	21	26	㉛	36	41				
Suzanne	①	4	7	10	13	⑯	19	22	25	28	㉛	34	37	40

They will be in the garden on the same day a total of three times in the next six weeks.

Grades 6-8

Iggy loves ice cream! His favorite flavor is caramel pecan swirl. His little sister, Izzy also loves ice cream. In fact, she loves every flavor! Last week, Iggy put a gallon of ice cream in the freezer. That night, Izzy ate half of the ice cream. The next night, she ate half of what was left. This continued for a total of six nights. On the seventh day, Iggy decided to have some of his ice cream. Boy, was he surprised when he opened the container! How much ice cream was left for Iggy? How much ice cream did Izzy eat?

Night	Amount in Fridge	Amount Izzy Eats	Amount Left
1	1 gallon	$\frac{1}{2}$ gallon	$\frac{1}{2}$ gallon
2	$\frac{1}{2}$ gallon	$\frac{1}{4}$ gallon	$\frac{1}{4}$ gallon
3	$\frac{1}{4}$ gallon	$\frac{1}{8}$ gallon	$\frac{1}{8}$ gallon
4	$\frac{1}{8}$ gallon	$\frac{1}{16}$ gallon	$\frac{1}{16}$ gallon
5	$\frac{1}{16}$ gallon	$\frac{1}{32}$ gallon	$\frac{1}{32}$ gallon
6	$\frac{1}{32}$ gallon	$\frac{1}{64}$ gallon	$\frac{1}{64}$ gallon

After six nights, there was $\frac{1}{64}$ gallon of ice cream left for Iggy. Izzy had eaten a total of $\frac{63}{64}$ gallons of ice cream.

Create an Organized List

Ready, Set, Solve (p. 99)

Grades K-2

How many different ways can you make 10 using addition with three addends?

*(**Note:** The order of the numbers doesn't matter. 3 + 3 + 4 is the same as 4 + 3 + 3)*

0 + 0 + 10	1 + 1 + 8	2 + 2 + 6	3 + 3 + 4
0 + 1 + 9	1 + 2 + 7	2 + 3 + 5	
0 + 2 + 8	1 + 3 + 6	2 + 4 + 4	
0 + 3 + 7	1 + 4 + 5		
0 + 4 + 6			
0 + 5 + 5			

There are 14 ways to make 10 using three addends.

Grades 3-5

Mark and Sara love pizza. They both like the following toppings on their pizza:

- *pepperoni*
- *chicken*
- *sausage*
- *pineapple*
- *mushrooms*
- *extra cheese*

They want to order and share a pizza, but they only have enough money for three toppings. How many different combinations are possible?

| P = pepperoni | M = mushrooms | PI = pineapple |
| S = sausage | C = chicken | CH = cheese |

P S M	S M C	C PI CH
P S C	S M PI	C PI M
P S PI	S M CH	C CH M
P S CH	S C PI	M CH PI
P M C	S C CH	
P M PI	S PI CH	
P M CH		
P C PI		
P C CH		
P PI CH		

There are 20 different pizzas with three toppings each.

Grades 6-8

Pat has a new bicycle lock. It's the kind that has a four-number combination. If the combination has four different numbers between 1 and 9 and all the numbers in the combination are even numbers, how many possible combinations would there be for Pat's lock?

2 4 6 8	4 2 6 8	6 2 4 8	8 2 4 6
2 4 8 6	4 2 8 6	6 2 8 4	8 2 6 4
2 6 4 8	4 6 2 8	6 4 2 8	8 4 2 6
2 6 8 4	4 6 8 2	6 4 8 2	8 4 6 2
2 8 4 6	4 8 2 6	6 8 2 4	8 6 2 4
2 8 6 4	4 8 6 2	6 8 4 2	8 6 4 2

There are 24 different combinations.

199

Guess and Check

Ready, Set, Solve (p. 102)

Grades K-2

When Matty emptied his piggy bank, he had nine coins, including pennies, nickels, and dimes. When he counted the value of the coins, he found he had 58¢. What coins did Matty have in his piggy bank?

dimes	5	4	4	5	5
nickels	3	4	3	2	1
pennies	1	1	2	2	3
total coins	9	9	9	9	9
total $	66¢	61¢	57¢	62¢	58¢

He had 5 dimes, 1 nickel, and 3 pennies.

Grades 3-5

The animal shelter has 10 more cats than dogs. They found homes for 2 cats and took in 2 dogs. Now there are twice as many cats as dogs. How many cats does the animal shelter have now?

cats	11	12	13	14
dogs	1	2	3	4
cats – 2	9	10	11	12
dogs + 2	3	4	5	6
twice as many cats?	no	no	no	yes

There are 12 cats in the shelter.

Grades 6-8

You have probably heard the tale of Ali Baba and the 40 thieves. I'll bet you never heard the story about his brother Bubba. One night, Bubba followed Ali and watched him enter the cave where they had hidden the stolen fortune. Later Bubba returned to the cave and spoke the magic words, Open Sesame. *The cave opened, and Bubba went inside. He was amazed to find 2,290 pounds of rubies and emeralds. There were four times as many 1-pound rubies as 3-pound rubies. He found three times as many 3-pound emeralds as 6-pound emeralds. How many rubies and how many emeralds of each size did Bubba Baba find in the cave?*

1 lb. Rubies	3 lb. Rubies	Ruby Weight	3 lb. Emeralds	6 lb. Emeralds	Emerald Weight	Total Weight
100	25	175	30	10	150	325
500	125	875	60	20	300	1,175
1,000	250	1750	90	30	450	2,200
1,500	375	2625	90	30	450	3,075
800	200	1400	120	40	600	2,000
900	225	1575	150	50	750	2,325
880	220	1540	150	50	750	2,290

Chapter 5

Using the Strategy (p. 107)

Make a Model

Look at the triangle below. Move exactly three pennies so that the triangle points down.

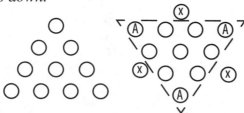

The three coins marked with an X are the coins to be moved. They can move to any of the spaces marked with an A.

Ready, Set, Solve (p. 109)

Grades K-2

Tonight's dinner includes peas and carrots. You HATE peas and carrots! Instead of eating the peas and carrots, you count them. You find out you have 12 vegetables on your plate. How many peas could you have? How many carrots could you have?

For this model, use green tiles (peas—shaded gray) and orange tiles (carrots—no shading). As you make a model, creating a table will help you keep track of your answers.

peas	carrots
1	11
2	10
3	9
4	8
5	7
6	6
7	5
8	4
9	3
10	2
11	1

Grades 3-5

How many ways can five squares be arranged so that the squares can only touch along a full side?

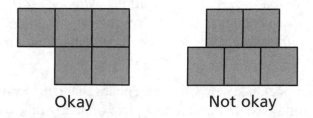

Okay   Not okay

Be careful of shapes that are rotations or reflections of pieces you have already found.

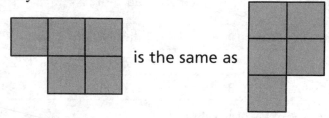

is the same as

Using tiles will help you find the possible shapes. Be careful to eliminate shapes that are reflections or rotations.

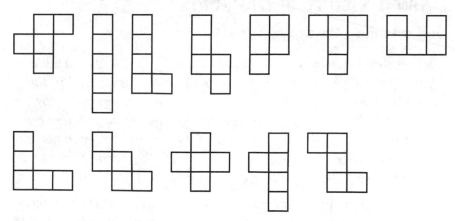

There are 12 possible arrangements of the tiles.

Grades 6-8

You want to make a container to hold some pebbles you have collected on the beach. All you have is a piece of cardboard that is 8" × 11". You decide to roll it into a cylinder. You can roll it horizontally, which is 11" tall, or vertically, which is 8" tall. If you want your container to hold the maximum amount of pebbles, which way should you roll the cardboard?

To make a model, take a piece of cardboard that is 8" × 11". Roll it lengthwise and tape it. Place it on a plate or pan. Fill it with rice or similar material. Remove the cylinder and take off the tape. Now roll it the other way and fill it with the rice you collected from the original cylinder. Which container held more?

Height	Circumference	Radius (C/2π)	Volume πr²(h)
8	11	1.751 in.	9.629 in.²
11	8	1.273 in.	5.093 in.²

The shorter cylinder holds more.

Draw a Picture or Diagram

Understanding the Strategy (p. 110)

Each evening, Larry takes his dog, Archie, for a walk. Archie is a very large dog. Every time they pass five houses, Archie turns around and pulls Larry back two houses. Then Larry pulls Archie forward five houses, and—you guessed it—Archie pulls Larry back two houses. If they need to walk past 20 houses in order to make it around the block and back to Larry's house, how many times will Larry have to pull Archie forward?

A 12-inch board was cut into two pieces so that the shorter piece was half as long as the larger piece. How long was the short piece?

Although either problem can be solved with a picture or diagram, the first problem is likely easier to be solved with a diagram because it has so many steps. The second problem can be solved with a picture.

Ready, Set, Solve (p. 113)

Grades K-2

Azziza invited 6 friends to her birthday party. Each person at the party received a cup with 5 chocolate candies and 2 sticks of gum. How many chocolate candies and how many sticks of gum were given at the party?

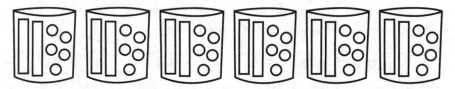

When you count the total number of chocolate candies and sticks of gum, there are 30 chocolate candies and 12 sticks of gum.

Grades 3-5

Ellen has season tickets to the ballpark. Her seat is in section 22. The row is second from the front and eighth from the back. Each row seats 15 people. How many seats are in section 22?

Begin drawing the location of Ellen's seat using the information in the problem.

Back

X
X
X
X
X
X
X
(X)
X

Front

From the drawing, I can tell there are nine rows of seats. Since each row has 15 seats, there are 9 × 15, or 135 seats in section 22.

Grades 6-8

Larry and Linda want to build a garden that will be placed right next to the garage. They have 100 yards of fencing to put around the garden to keep out the rabbits. They would like to make the largest rectangular garden possible. All of the sides must be whole numbers. Determine the best size for the garden.

Begin with a drawing that will fit the information in the problem. Keeping a table as you adjust the dimensions of the garden will help you find the garden with the greatest area.

length	width	perimeter	area
10 yd.	40 yd.	100 yd.	400 yd.^{2}
11 yd.	38 yd.	98 yd.	418 yd.^{2}
12 yd.	36 yd.	96 yd.	432 yd.^{2}
13 yd.	34 yd.	94 yd.	442 yd.^{2}
14 yd.	32 yd.	92 yd.	448 yd.^{2}
15 yd.	30 yd.	90 yd.	450 yd.^{2}
16 yd.	28 yd.	88 yd.	448 yd.^{2}
17 yd.	26 yd.	86 yd.	442 yd.^{2}

Notice that the area begins to decrease after 15×30. So 15×30 is the best size for the garden. The area will be 450 sq yd.

Act It Out

Ready, Set, Solve (p. 116)

Grades K-2

Marcy puts coins in her piggy bank every week. There is a total of 50¢ in the piggy bank. What coins could she have if there are six coins in the piggy bank? seven coins? eight coins?

Get some coins and act this out. Notice that you will also be using some of the other strategies. Guess and Check and Create a Table will help you to keep track of your work.

Do not give up when you have found one solution. There may be more than one way to solve the problem. Try using the coins to make combinations that equal 50¢.

4 coins

5 coins

6 coins

6 coins

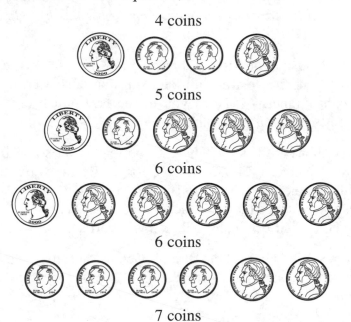

7 coins

If you exchange a dime for two nickels, you can make 50¢ with seven coins using three dimes and four nickels.

8 coins

If you exchange another dime for two nickels, you can make 50¢ using two dimes and six nickels.

Grades 3-5

Darren bought a bike for $50. Later that summer, he sold it to his friend Dennis for $60. He bought it back for $70 and then sold it for $80. Did he earn or lose money, and how much? Or did he come out even?

Before you act this out, think about the problem and write down what you think the answer will be. You may also want to work it out with numbers—it helps you to see how much clearer the situation is when you act it out.

Get some money—it doesn't have to be real! Get some friends, a bike (or a picture of a bike) and go for it. By the way, students love this problem! Don't tell them the answer—under any circumstances. Once they have acted it out, they will be convinced as to whether their original prediction was correct.

So, you need the bike seller, Darren, Dennis, and the bike buyer. Each person should start with $200. Act out the steps in the problem:

Darren buys the bike for $50.

He sells it to Dennis for $60.

He buys it back for $70.

He sells it again for $80.

Now have each person count his money. How much does Darren have at the end of all of the transactions? If you count $220, you can see that he made $20.

A good follow-up once the problem has been acted out is to think of how you will represent the actions of the problem in showing your work.

Grades 6-8

You are having a birthday party. When the first person arrives, you shake her hand. As each new guest arrives, he or she shakes hands with everyone at the party. There is a total of 10 people at the party. If each person shakes hands with everyone else exactly one time, how many handshakes will there be?

There are several ways to act out this problem. First you need to understand exactly what is happening. Each person shakes hands with each other person exactly once. So, once I shake your hand, I don't touch it again.

Get a group of 10 people. Determine how you will act out the problem so that every person shakes every other person's hand once. One way to do this is to have everyone line up. The first person goes down the line and shakes 9 hands—and he or she is now out of the line. The second person goes down the line and shakes 8 hands—and he or she is now out of the line. This continues with the third person shaking 7 hands and with every other person shaking hands until 1 person is left standing—since he or she has already shaken everyone else's hand, he or she shakes 0 hands. Do you see the pattern?

$$9 + 8 + 7 + 6 + 5 + 4 + 3 + 2 + 1 + 0 = 45 \text{ handshakes}$$

Create or Use a Graph

Understanding the Strategy (p. 117)

The 30 fifth-graders at Euclid Elementary School are planning their class party. They have taken a survey of pizza toppings. Of the students, 17 want pepperoni on their pizza and 21 of them want mushrooms. There are two vegetarians in the class who will only have cheese. Of all the students, how many want both pepperoni and mushrooms on their pizza? Use a Venn diagram to help solve the problem.

This problem can be solved with a variety of different strategies. Using a Venn diagram is a good way to organize your work, to check to be sure that it fits the information in the problem, and to represent your thinking. With the Venn diagram, you can also use materials such as markers to represent the students. Move the markers around until you have reached a solution.

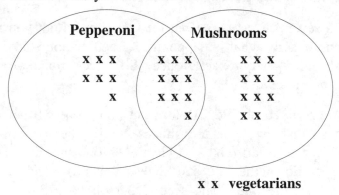

There are 10 students who want pepperoni and mushrooms.

Ready, Set, Solve (p. 119)

Grades K-2

The second graders are playing a dice game. They roll two dice, add the numbers, and move that number of spaces on the game board. Fred is wondering which sum comes up the most often when you roll two dice. So, the kids decide to collect some data to find out. Roll two dice 50 times, and use a graph to keep track of the rolls. How would you answer Fred's question?

To solve this problem, you need to roll two dice, add the number on each, and keep track of your sums in a graph. If you use this problem with your students, you may need to set up the graph before they begin to work. What sums are possible? Now, roll the dice 50 times and record each outcome on the graph. A sample graph is shown on the next page. What conclusions can you draw from the results?

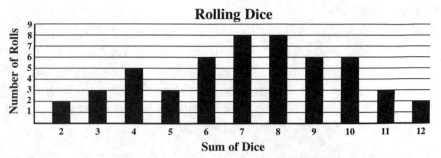

Rolling Dice

The sums of 7 and 8 occur most often. Note that with 50 rolls, results may vary considerably. Combining student data to include more trials will get closer to the actual probability, which is the sum of 7 occurring the most often.

Grades 3-5

The new Bouncy Ball is quite special. Each time the ball bounces, it bounces half as high as the time before. The ball is dropped from a tower that is 128 feet tall. It is caught when it bounces up 1 foot. How many times did the ball hit the ground before it is caught?

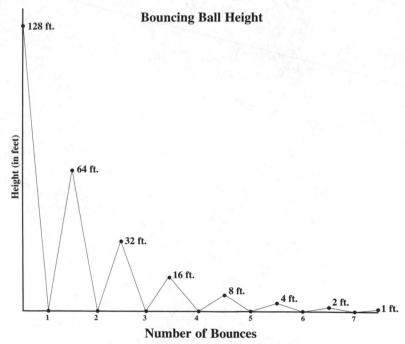

Bouncing Ball Height

The ball will bounce 7 times before it is caught.

Grades 6-8

The Lincoln Middle School Basketball team has 14 players. They are listed at three positions: forward, center, and guard. When the manager counts the centers and guards, she counts 8 players. When she counts the forwards and the centers, she counts 9 players. How many centers, how many forwards, and how many guards are on the team?

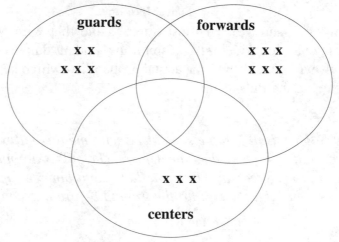

There are 5 guards, 6 forwards, and 3 centers.

Chapter 6

Solve a Simpler Problem

Using the Strategy (p. 123)

Find the sum of the first 50 odd numbers.

Simplify: Begin by finding the sum of the first 2 odd numbers.

$1 + 3 = 4$

Move on to the first three odd numbers, then the first four odd numbers.

$1 + 3 + 5 = 9$

$1 + 3 + 5 + 7 = 16$.

Keep track of your work and continue until you notice a pattern. Once you notice a pattern, you can continue to increase the number of addends, or if you can generalize the pattern, you can jump to 50 addends. In fact, you can then solve this problem for any number of addends!

$1 + 3 = 4$

$1 + 3 + 5 = 9$

$1 + 3 + 5 + 7 = 16$

$1 + 3 + 5 + 7 + 9 = 25$

$1 + 3 + 5 + 7 + 9 + 11 = 36$

$1 + 3 + 5 + 7 + 9 + 11 + 13 = 49$

Notice that the sum in each equation is a square number.

$$1 + 3 = 4 \ (2 \times 2)$$

$$1 + 3 + 5 = 9 \ (3 \times 3)$$

$$1 + 3 + 5 + 7 = 16 \ (4 \times 4)$$

$$1 + 3 + 5 + 7 + 9 = 25 \ (5 \times 5)$$

$$1 + 3 + 5 + 7 + 9 + 11 = 36 \ (6 \times 6)$$

$$1 + 3 + 5 + 7 + 9 + 11 + 13 = 49 \ (7 \times 7)$$

Can you predict what the next sum will be?

Look more closely.

Can you determine what number will be squared by looking at the addition equation?

Predict the sum of the first 10 odd numbers.

Did you notice that the number of addends is the same as the number you are squaring?

So, the sum of the first 10 odd numbers is 10^2 or 100.

With this pattern, you should be able to generalize the sum of the first 50 odd numbers. ($50 \times 50 = 2,500$)

A football team of 12 players must choose a captain and a co-captain. How many different combinations are possible?

Simplify: How many combinations would be possible for a team with three players? four players?

Making a tree diagram will help to keep track of the possibilities. Can you find the pattern? Can you determine the answer to this problem without having to do every case by extending the pattern?

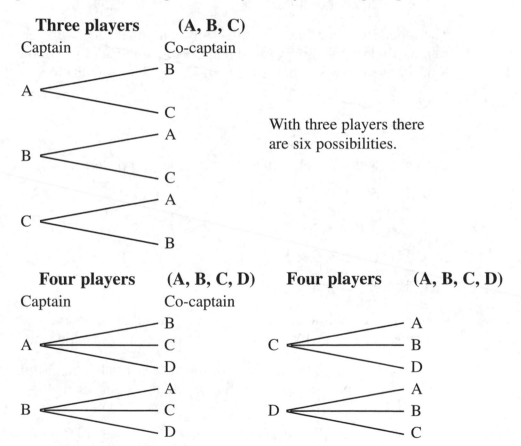

Three players **(A, B, C)**

Captain

Co-captain

With three players there are six possibilities.

Four players **(A, B, C, D)** **Four players** **(A, B, C, D)**

Captain

Co-captain

With four players there are 12 possibilities.

Continue the tree diagrams until you think you have the pattern and can identify the number of combinations for 12 players.

The pattern:

Each of 3 players can match up with the other two players, so $3 \times 2 = 6$ combinations.

Each of 4 players can match up with the other three players, so $4 \times 3 = 12$ combinations.

Each of 5 players can match up with the other four players, so $5 \times 4 = 20$ combinations.

The pattern continues with any number of players so $n \times (n - 1)$ would give you the number of combinations. For the football team, it would be $12 \times 11 = 132$ possible combinations.

Find the product:

$5^5 \times 5^8$

Let's start with a simpler situation and look for a pattern.

$5^1 \times 5^1 = 5 \times 5 = 5^2$

$5^1 \times 5^2 = 5 \times 5 \times 5 = 5^3$

$5^2 \times 5^2 = 5 \times 5 \times 5 \times 5 = 5^4$

$5^2 \times 5^3 = 5 \times 5 \times 5 \times 5 \times 5 = 5^5$

Continue with additional examples until you find the pattern. Can you generalize a rule for multiplying any numbers with exponents?

The exponent indicates how many times 5 is used as a factor. Notice if you add the exponents, this will tell you how many times to multiply 5.

Therefore $5^5 \times 5^8 = 5^{13}$

Ready, Set, Solve (p. 127)

Grades K-2

Miranda loves to count. On her way to school today, she counted these things:

- *One white kitten sitting on the front porch.*
- *Two frogs hopping across the street.*
- *Three robins singing in the tree.*
- *Four grasshoppers jumping along the sidewalk.*
- *Five poodles going for a walk.*
- *Six squirrels climbing up the trees.*
- *Seven fire hydrants painted red.*
- *Eight daffodils swaying in the wind.*
- *Nine pine trees with pine cones hanging low.*
- *Ten acorns sitting on the ground.*

How many things did Miranda count altogether?

Begin with the kitten and frog.

$1 + 2 = 3$

Now add on the 4 grasshoppers.

$3 + 4 = 7$

Continue with each set of items until you have added $1 + 2 + 3 + 4 + 5 + 6 + 7 + 8 + 9 + 10$.

Miranda counted 55 items on her way to school.

Grades 3-5

Tony's restaurant has 30 small tables to be used for a banquet. Each table can seat only one person on each side. If the tables are pushed together to make one long table, how many people can sit at the table?

Start with a simpler problem and draw pictures to demonstrate what is happening.

	x	
x	☐	x 1 table seats 4 people
	x	

tables	people	
1	4	
2	6	+2
3	8	+2
4	10	+2

x   x
x ☐☐ x   2 tables seat 6 people
x   x

x x x
x ☐☐☐ x   3 tables seat 8 people
x x x

Each time you add a table, you add two more people. You could continue the table by adding 2 each time, but that is a lot of work!

Look at the pictures you drew. What do you notice?

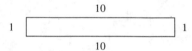

What would 10 tables look like?

What would 20 tables look like?

Can you use this pattern to figure out what 30 tables would look like?

$30 + 30 + 1 + 1 = 62$ people

Grades 6-8

How many squares of any size are on a standard 8 × 8 checkerboard?

The simplest problem to start with is a 1 × 1 checkerboard.

there is 1 square

In a 2 × 2 checkerboard, there are two different size squares.

four small and one large

219

In a 3 × 3 checkerboard, there are three different size squares.

nine small, four medium, and one large

size	squares	total
1 × 1	■ 1	1 square
2 × 2	■ 4 ■ 1	5 squares
3 × 3	■ 9 ■ 4 ■ 1	14 squares
4 × 4	■ 16 ■ 9 ■ 4 ■ 1	30 squares

How many different sizes are in a 4 × 4 checkerboard?

If you complete the table, you can find the pattern for the number of squares in an 8 × 8 checkerboard.

In an 8 × 8 checkerboard, there are

$$64 + 49 + 36 + 25 + 16 + 9 + 4 + 1 \text{ or } 204 \text{ squares.}$$

Account for All Possibilities

Using the Strategy (p. 129)

Francine went to the store to buy some fruit. She can get 3 oranges for 50¢. She has lots of coins but no half dollars and no pennies. Find all of the combinations of coins she could use to pay for the oranges.

Quarters	Dimes	Nickels
2	0	0
1	2	1
1	1	3
1	0	5
0	5	0
0	4	2
0	3	4
0	2	6
0	1	8
0	0	10

How can you be sure that you've found all of the possible combinations of coins?

There are some very strange creatures on the planet Mathoid. Some creatures have two eyes and some have three eyes. On my last visit, I counted a total of 23 eyes. How many of each creature did I meet on Mathoid?

This is a great problem because there is more than one possible solution. Let's make a table to keep track of our work. Once you've determined the number of two-eyed creatures, how can you figure out the number of three-eyed creatures?

2 eyes	1	2	3	3	4	5	6	6	7	8	9	9	10	11
3 eyes	7	6	6	5	5	4	4	3	3	2	2	1	1	1
total	23	22	24	21	23	22	24	21	23	22	24	21	23	25
solution?	yes	no	no	no	yes	no	no	no	yes	no	no	no	yes	no

I could have met 1 creature with two eyes and 7 creatures with three eyes; or 4 creatures with two eyes and 5 creatures with three eyes; or 7 creatures with two eyes and 3 creatures with three eyes; or 10 creatures with two eyes and 1 creature with three eyes.

How can you be sure that we have accounted for all of the possibilities?

Mark and his father are putting up a fence in their back yard. Some sections are 15 feet long, and the others are 18 feet long. What is the least number of sections they can put up so that the fence is 270 feet long? How many of each will they use?

Let's create a table to keep track of our work.

15-foot Pieces	Length of 15-foot Pieces	Remainder of Length Needed	Divisible by 18?
1	15	255	no
2	30	240	no
3	45	225	no
4	60	210	no
5	75	195	no
6	90	180	yes

This could be done with 16 sections. Mark and his father need six 15-foot pieces and ten 8-foot sections. There are other combinations that will work, but this requires the least amount of sections.

Ready, Set, Solve (p. 130)

Grades K-2

Rachelle's house number has three different digits.

The sum of the three digits is 12.

The number is greater than 480.

What could the house number be?

Do you think you found all the possible solutions?

Since the house number is greater than 480, the digit in the hundreds place has to be greater than 4. You also know that the digits add to 12. Now you can get started. Look for combinations that add to 12. You need to eliminate solutions with digits that are the same.

507	~~606~~	705	804	903
516	615	714	813	912
~~525~~	624	723	~~822~~	921
534	~~633~~	732	831	930
543	642	741	840	
552	651	750		
561	~~660~~			
570				

There are 25 possible addresses for Rachelle's house.

Grades 3-5

Mrs. Fairweather has placed 12 tiles in a bag. Some are red, some are blue, and some are yellow. There are no other colors. How many different combinations of tiles are possible?

Let's use a table to organize our work.

Red	Blue	Yellow		Red	Blue	Yellow
10	1	1		3	8	1
9	2	1		3	7	2
9	1	2		3	6	3
8	3	1		3	5	4
8	2	2		3	4	5
8	1	3		3	3	6
7	4	1		3	2	7
7	3	2		3	1	8
7	2	3		2	9	1
7	1	4		2	8	2
6	5	1		2	7	3
6	4	2		2	6	4
6	3	3		2	5	5
6	2	4		2	4	6
6	1	5		2	3	7
5	6	1		2	2	8
5	5	2		2	1	9
5	4	3		1	10	1
5	3	4		1	9	2
5	2	5		1	8	3
5	1	6		1	7	4
4	7	1		1	6	5
4	6	2		1	5	6
4	5	3		1	4	7
4	4	4		1	3	8
4	3	5		1	2	9
4	2	6		1	1	10
4	1	7				

This table shows all of the possible solutions. Recognizing patterns as the table is constructed will help you solve the problem more efficiently. Can you find the patterns?

Grades 6-8

Mutt and Jeff are playing a game with the spinner shown here. They spin twice and add the fractions. If the sum is greater than $\frac{1}{2}$, Jeff gets a point. If the sum is less than $\frac{1}{2}$, Mutt gets a point. Is the game fair? Explain your reasoning.

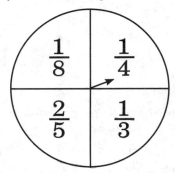

Here are the possible combinations:

$\frac{1}{8} + \frac{1}{8} = \frac{1}{4}$ $\frac{1}{8} + \frac{1}{3} = \frac{11}{24}$ $\frac{1}{8} + \frac{2}{5} = \frac{21}{40}$ $\frac{1}{8} + \frac{1}{4} = \frac{3}{8}$

$\frac{1}{4} + \frac{1}{4} = \frac{1}{2}$ $\frac{1}{4} + \frac{1}{3} = \frac{7}{12}$ $\frac{1}{4} + \frac{2}{5} = \frac{13}{20}$

$\frac{2}{5} + \frac{2}{5} = \frac{4}{5}$ $\frac{2}{5} + \frac{1}{3} = \frac{11}{15}$

$\frac{1}{3} + \frac{1}{3} = \frac{2}{3}$

Theoretical probability shows that there is a 60% chance that the sum is greater than $\frac{1}{2}$. The sum is less than $\frac{1}{2}$ 30% of the time and equal to $\frac{1}{2}$ 10% of the time. Thus, the game is not fair. Jeff has a higher probability of winning the game.

Work Backwards

Using the Strategy (p. 131)

Kenny took some money out of his bank. He spent 50¢ at the store and had $1.75 left. How much money did he have to begin with?

$\_\_\_\_\_ - \$0.50 = \$1.75$

In order to determine what he had to start with, you would have to put the 50¢ back, or add it to the $1.75.

$1.75 + $0.50 = $2.25

It is always a good idea to check the solution by working the problem "forward" to be certain that you have correctly reversed all of the actions.

Does $2.25 − $0.50 = $1.75? It checks, so the solution of $2.25 must be correct.

Last night Mom baked some blueberry muffins for our class picnic. Much to my surprise, my brother ate ¼ of the muffins. My dad ate ⅔ of what was left. Then my little sister found the plate of muffins and ate ½ of what was left. When I went to get the muffins, there were only two left. How many muffins did Mom bake?

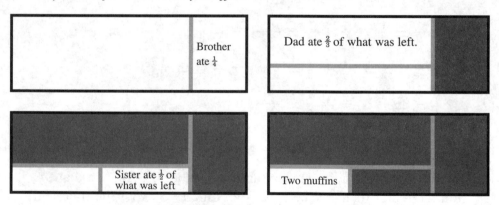

Final Step

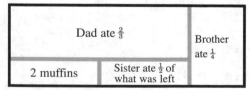

If you know the amount that is 2 muffins, can you determine how many muffins each person ate?

If the final box represents 2 muffins, that means that Sister ate 2 muffins because she ate the same amount as what was left. Dad ate

4 times as much as Sister. That gives a total of 12 muffins which is $\frac{3}{4}$ of the total muffins. If 12 muffins are $\frac{3}{4}$, than 4 muffins is $\frac{1}{4}$. So there were 12 + 4, or 16 muffins to start.

Let's check:

16 muffins to start

Brother takes $\frac{1}{4}$ of 16, or 4 muffins. That leaves 12 muffins.

Dad takes $\frac{2}{3}$ of 12, or 8 muffins. That leaves 4 muffins.

Sister takes $\frac{1}{2}$ of 4, or 2 muffins. That leaves 2 muffins. That means there must have been 16 muffins to start.

Ready, Set, Solve (p. 133)

Grades K-2

Patrick shook the coins out of his piggy bank. He took 25¢ to buy a cool pencil for school. He took 15¢ to buy an eraser. When he counted the money that was left, he still had 45¢. How much money did Patrick have in his bank before he took the coins?

_____ – 25¢ – 15¢ = 45¢

If you add 15¢ back to 45¢, that makes 60¢. That is what Patrick had before he bought the eraser. Now add back the 25¢ for the pencil, and you'll see that he had 85¢ in his bank to start.

Let's check:

85¢ –25¢ = 60¢ and 60¢ – 15¢ = 45¢. Patrick had 45¢ left after he made his purchases, so we are correct that he started with 85¢.

Grades 3-5

Mom just filled the cookie jar with cookies. They were chocolate-chunk cookies—my favorite. My brother came home from soccer practice and took ½ the cookies. My sister came home from dance lessons and took half of what was left. When my dad got home from work, he took half the remaining cookies. By the time I finished my homework and went downstairs for a snack, there were only two cookies left. How many cookies did Mom put in the cookie jar?

We can solve this problem by working backwards with a diagram.

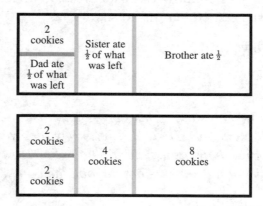

Mom put 16 cookies in the jar.

Grades 6-8

Dorothy and Toto were on the yellow brick road with a full basket of oranges. When she met the Scarecrow he was very hungry, so she gave him half her oranges plus two more. Later, she met the Tin Man and gave him half of the remaining oranges plus two more. And when she met the Lion, she gave him half the remaining oranges plus two more. When they arrived in Oz, Dorothy had two oranges left in her basket. How many oranges were in the basket before Dorothy gave any away?

Dorothy had two oranges when she arrived in Oz.

She gave the Lion ½ her oranges plus two more. So she had to take back the two more. She then had four oranges. Double the four

228

oranges (since she gave the Tin Man half), and that means she had eight oranges before she met the Lion.

After she met the Tin Man, she had 8 oranges left. She had given the Tin Man half her oranges plus two more. Put back the two she gave him, so that she has 10. Double the 10 oranges, since she gave him half, and that means she had 20 oranges before she met the Tin Man.

After she met the Scarecrow, she had 20 oranges left. She gave the Scarecrow half her oranges plus two more. Put back the two she gave him, so that she has 22. Double the 22 oranges, since she gave him half, which means she had 44 oranges before she met the Scarecrow.

Let's check.

Dorothy starts with 44 oranges. She gives the Scarecrow half plus two more (22 + 2), which leaves her with 20 oranges. She gives the Tin Man half plus two more (10 + 2), which leaves her with eight oranges. She gives the Lion half plus two more (4 + 2), which leaves her with two oranges. So Dorothy has just two oranges when she arrives in Oz.

Change Your Point of View

Using the Strategy (p. 136)

Toothpick Puzzles

Remove one toothpick to leave 3 squares.

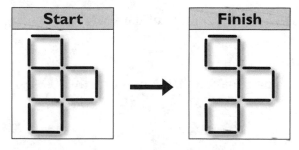

Toothpick Puzzles *(cont.)*

Make this figure with 12 toothpicks.

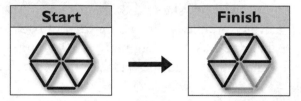

1. Remove four toothpicks and leave three triangles.

2. Move four toothpicks and form three triangles.

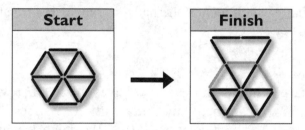

Word Jumbles

Rearrange the letters to make a mathematical word.

nidodait	addition
rgatinel	triangle

Sequences

Complete the following sequence:

J, F, M, A, M, J, J, A, S, <u>O</u> , <u>N</u> , <u>D</u>

(the initial letter of each month of the year)

Brain Teasers

Use four 9s in an equation that equals exactly 100.

$$99 + \frac{9}{9} = 100$$

Mathematical Puzzles

Arrange 10 trees in five rows, with four trees in each row. (• = tree)

Mathematical Riddles

- Which weighs more: A pound of iron or a pound of feathers?
  Neither—they both weigh one pound.

- Why should you never mention the number 288 in front of anyone?
  Because it's too gross! (2 × 144 = 288 and 144 is one gross)

- A street that is 40 yards long has a tree every 10 yards on both sides. How many total trees on the entire street?
  There are 10 trees—5 on each side of the street

Ready, Set, Solve (p. 138)

Grades K-2

Arrange eight toothpicks in the shape of a fish. Move toothpicks until the fish is facing another direction. How many toothpicks did you move? Can you do it another way? What is the least number of toothpicks you can move?

Example:

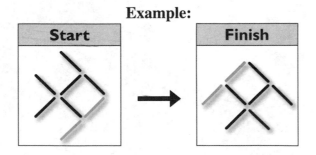

The fewest number of toothpicks that can be moved is 2.

Grades 3-5

Complete each of the following sequences.

S, M, T, W, T, __F__, __S__ (days of the week)

O, T, T, F, F, __S__, __S__, __E__ (counting numbers)

F, S, T, F, F, S, S, __E__, __N__, __T__ (ordinal numbers)

M, V, E, M, J, S, __U__, __N__ (planets in order from the sun)

Grade 6-8

A farmer, a fox, a chicken, and a bag of corn must safely cross the river in a very small boat. The farmer may only take one thing at a time in the boat. She cannot leave the fox and the chicken together on either side of the river, or the fox will eat the chicken. And, she cannot leave the chicken alone with the bag of corn, or the chicken will eat the corn. How can the farmer get everything across the river without anything being eaten?

Shore	River	Shore
fox and corn	farmer takes chicken ➡	
fox and corn	farmer returns ⬅	chicken
corn	farmer takes fox ➡	chicken
corn	farmer returns with chicken ⬅	fox
chicken	farmer takes corn ➡	fox
chicken	farmer returns ⬅	fox and corn
	farmer takes chicken ➡	farmer, chicken, fox, and corn

Additional Problem Solutions

Chapter 3

1.

	3-quart pail	5-quart pail	8-quart pail	
start	3	5	0	
	0	5	3	empty the 3-quart pail into the 8-quart pail
	3	2	3	fill the 3-quart pail from the 5-quart pail
	0	2	6	empty the 3-quart pail into the 8-quart pail
	2	0	6	empty the 5-quart pail into the 3-quart pail
	2	5	1	fill the 5-quart pail from the 8-quart pail
	3	4	1	fill the 3-quart pail with 1 quart from the 5-quart pail
	0	4	4	empty the 3-quart pail into the 8-quart pail

2. Each person should pay $6.00. Ricardo owes $1.00. Marina owes $4.00. Mina should get $2.00 back, and Dave should get $3.00 back.

3. She took the radio back 36 times.

4. George placed first. Jacob was second. Jonathan and Josh tied for third place, and Jason came in last.

5. Nihal polled 58 people: there were 22 football fans; there were 33 baseball fans; there were five who liked both football and baseball; there were eight who did not like either sport.

6. Ruth has 4 blue markers, 3 red markers, and 5 green markers.

7. It would take 5,815 toothpicks.

8. The area of the 8-plot garden is 64 square units, and the perimeter is 46 units.

9. He would have to shovel snow for 9 hours.

10. The house number is 594.

Chapter 4

1. Lashay has 93 pennies.

2. I am 56.

3. Bozo has 1 half dollar, 1 quarter, 3 dimes and 2 pennies.

4. The 100th number in the sequence is 298.

5. The concert was attended by 400 people.

6. 70, 72, 74
   51, 53, 55, 57
   71, 72, 73

7. There will be 90 golf balls not sold.

8. He will rescue the maiden on the 11th day.

9. TD = touchdown   FG = field goal
PA = point after   SA = safety

TD (6)	PA (1)	FG (3)	SA (2)
2	1	0	1
2	0	1	0
1	1	2	1
1	1	0	4
1	0	3	0
1	0	1	3
0	0	5	0
0	0	3	3
0	0	1	6

10. They will swim on the 21st day and play baseball on the 31st day.

11. There are many solutions to this problem. Here is one:

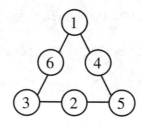

Chapter 5

1. They both ate the same amount.

2. She baked 196 cookies.

3. There are many possible solutions to this problem.
Check to be sure your solution matches the clues.

4. It takes him 6 days. When he reaches the top, he climbs out, so he doesn't slide back.

5. He should trade 18 peanuts.

6. It is physically impossible to fold a paper in half 10 times, but if you could, there would be 1,024 layers of paper.

7. The explorer spotted 10 animals with both fur and a tail.

8. They will be at the pool on the same day 4 times.

9. The children are 2, 2, and 9.

10. Snow White sent the letter to Nosy.

Chapter 6

1. There are 28 different rectangles.

2. She would have to get up at 7:20 A.M.

3. She could have 1 penny, 2 nickels, and 5 dimes (61¢) or 1 penny, 3 nickels, and 4 dimes (56¢).

4. She cut the chocolate bar into 36 pieces.

5. Caleb received $34 for his allowance.

6. You would have to knock down 55 pins.

7. Alex would receive a total of $163.84 on the 15th day.

8. Marvin baked 16 brownies.

9. There were 18 grapes in the basket.

10. 10¢. You can do it with 2 cuts.

References

Burns, M. 2007. *About teaching mathematics*. Math Solutions: Sausalito, CA.

Chief Council of State School Officers. 2010. Formative assessment for students and teachers. http://www.ccsso.org/Resources/Programs/Formative_Assessment_for_Students_and_Teachers_%28FAST%29.html. (Accessed February 1, 2011.)

Common Core State Standards. 2010. http://corestandards.org/the-standards. (Accessed January, 31, 2011.)

Fitzgerald, W., G. Lappan, G. D. Phillips, J. Shroyer, and M. J. Winter. 1986. *The middle grades mathematics project*. Addison-Wesley Publishing Company: Boston, MA.

Heibert, J., K. C. Fuson, D. Wearne, and E. Fennema. 1997. *Making sense: Teaching and learning mathematics with understanding*. Heinemann: Portsmouth, NH.

Kroll, V. 2005. *Equal shmequal*. Charlesbridge Publishing: Watertown, MA.

Lester, F. 2003. *Teaching mathematics through problem solving*. NCTM: Reston, VA.

National Council of Teachers of Mathematics (NCTM). 2000. *Principles and standards for school mathematics*. NCTM: Reston, VA.

National Governors Association for Best Practices (NGABS) and Council of Chief State School Officers (CCSSO). 2010. *Common core state standards*. http://corestandards.org/the-standards/mathematics. (Accessed November 19, 2010.)

National Research Council. 2001. *Adding it up: Helping children learn mathematics*. Ed. J. Kilpatric, J. Swafford, and B. Findell. Mathematics Learning Study Committee, Center for Education, Division of Behavioral and Social Sciences and Education. Washington DC: National Academy Press

Polya, G. 2009. *How to solve it: A new aspect of mathematical method*. Ishi Press: Japan.

Van de Walle, J., K. Karp, and J. Bay-Williams. 2009. *Elementary and middle school mathematics: Teaching developmentally*. Allyn & Bacon: Upper Saddle Lake, NJ.